Tribal Unity

Getting From Teams to Tribes by Creating a One Team Culture

Em Campbell-Pretty

First published in 2016 by Pretty Agile Pty Ltd
Richmond, Victoria, Australia

© Pretty Agile Pty Ltd
The moral rights of the author have been asserted.
This book is a SpiritCast Network Book

National Library of Australia Cataloguing-in-Publication data:

Author:
>   Campbell-Pretty, Em
Title:
>   Tribal Unity: Getting From Teams to Tribes by Creating a One Team
>   Culture
ISBN-13:
>   978-1537347578
ISBN 10:
>   1537347578
Subjects:
>   1. Teams in the workplace. 2. Leadership. 3. Organisational Behaviour. 4.
>   Organisational Effectiveness

Editor-in-chief: Anita Saunders

Cover Design: Bliss Inventive

Disclaimer:
The material in this publication is of the nature of general comment only, and does not represent professional advice. It is not intended to provide specific guidance for particular circumstances and it should not be relied on as the basis for any decision to take action or not take action on any matter which it covers. Readers should obtain professional advice where appropriate, before making any such decision. To the maximum extent permitted by law, the author and publisher disclaim all responsibility and liability to any person, arising directly or indirectly from any person taking or not taking action based on the information in this publication.

Praise for *Tribal Unity*

"What executive wouldn't want a highly productive group, capable of taking on big, strategic projects with aggressive timelines? What employee wouldn't want a workplace that inspires—with camaraderie, fun, worthy challenges, AND genuine management support? Up until now, these two desires have seemed mutually exclusive, and elusive.

In *Tribal Unity*, Em shows that it is possible to have both, and indeed, latter enables the former. Em is no starry-eyed dreamer. She's a business manager and knows what is at stake. This book is full of examples, stories, practices, and practical advice. She shows you that productivity + joy is not pie-in-the-sky, but well within the achievable."

- Esther Derby, co-author of
Agile Retrospectives: Making Good Teams Great and
Behind Closed Doors: Secrets of Great Management

"Succeeding in building a strong tribe - a team of teams - is one of the keys to unlocking potential in your organization beyond the individual team. But how do you do that in practice? Most books only tackle this with principles or abstract concepts - but in this book Em describes real, concrete practices illustrated through her own experiences that will not only inspire you to build a stronger tribe, but also guide you in how to do it."

- Anders Ivarsson, Organizational Coach, Spotify

"Every aspiring Lean-Agile enterprise can be no better than the culture that evolves to support it. Em does a great job of describing how that culture can be fostered directly with the "team-of-agile-teams", the essential building block of enterprise agility."

- Dean Leffingwell, creator of the
Scaled Agile Framework

"*Tribal Unity* is a must read for leaders needing to get their teams together to get the work done that needs to be done. It connects us to contemporary thinking; real life examples are backed up with quotes and insights from relevant readings and other industry leaders.

We gain from Em's lessons learnt and these are passed on to us in her easy style with humour and pragmatic language. Her voice is strong in reading in each page; it's true to her and it's oh-so useful for us.

There are plenty of daily tips and techniques coupled with practical advice of what to do. I think it will revolutionise how you lead - and how you think you can lead - a team towards being a tribe.

It's a beautiful bringing together of agile, culture and people - to create tribes that people want to be a part of."

- Lynne Cazaly author of
Leader as Facilitator, Making Sense,
Create Change and Visual Mojo

"I have long been an admirer of the work that Em does in building great teams and great tribes. This book is a perfect distillation of a lot of very sound advice on creating teams that hum. Drawing on real life experiences and backing them up with solid principles, *Tribal Unity* is a must-read for anyone who leads or wants to lead a tribe. Em has great stories to tell and I find myself retelling them to colleagues and friends as inspiration and as practical advice; I'm glad that they're collected in a single book that I can recommend to people as a manual on how to transform an organisation."

- Andy Kelk, CTO, Marketplacer

"Em tells a very personal and human story about how to create awesome tribes. Her book is full of useful take-aways, real life examples and practical ideas people can use. One big lesson shared is that success if often based on having the courage to seize opportunities. Even seasoned Agilists will find something here! I certainly did."

- **Sandy Mamoli, co-author *Creating Great Teams:***
How Self-Selection Lets People Excel

"*Tribal Unity* by Em Campbell-Pretty, is the finest guidebook for today's evolving organizations dedicated to transforming workplaces into cultures of competency and fun!

Using real-world and witty anecdotes, Em's years of experience as a curator of change fosters a fresh perspective on nurturing teams by applying Lean Agile principles to a corporate environment.

Em takes a commanding approach to moving from average to excellent. All the while, she leans on her natural sense of humor and insight to keep teams and individuals engaged and safe, providing effective approaches to connect with a common goal."

- **Lynn Winterboer,**
Agile Analytics Coach & Trainer

"Em's is the first true and authentic voice in the Scaling Agile space. Rather than sell you on grand unifying theories and ideas, she tells her own story of personal, team and organisational development. *Tribal Unity* documents Em's journey leaving a trail bread crumbs (books and articles) for others to follow. Its so refreshing to see how her thoughts developed around solving the problems rather than selling the solutions. I'm utterly jealous that I haven't written such a rich, poetic and useful book as Tribal Unity. - Jealous of London"

- **Chris Matts, Agile Transformation Coach, Co-Author of**
***Commitment*, and Co-inventor of the**
Given-When-Then syntax.

"Too many "teams" never really gel. With no shared culture, they either storm in friction, or become micro-fiefdoms, led by a handful of strong personalities. As the teams grow, the friction gets worse. Eventually, you realize that ten dedicated people could do what this group of fifty is struggling to accomplish, perhaps in less time!

The culture problem is something that by-the-book Scrum doesn't solve. You need something deeper - exercises, communication patterns, and models to understand what is going on, find the friction points, and allow the team to gel. Most of the advice in this area is shallow. A tip here, a tidbit there. Em Campbell-Pretty's book, *Tribal Unity*, breaks new ground by combining sound advice with her own personal experience and insights. Combine that with pictures of real artifacts and examples, and you have the making of something new. If your company norms need work, or you don't have them, read this book. If you don't, read it anyway, you'll need it at the next assignment."

- Matthew Heusser, Managing Director,
Excelon Development

"Em's breakout book is an insightful and practical narrative on the structure and leadership of teams. Whether you lead one team or one hundred, you will learn something new about creating unity of purpose."

- Evan Leybourn, author of
Directing the Agile Organisation

"Simply put, *Tribal Unity* was written from genuine hands-on experience. It doesn't contain fluffy theory but rather hard-hitting real-world anecdotes and case studies making it refreshing and a pleasure to read. Credit goes to Em for sharing with us all her well-earned stripes!"

- Ilan Goldstein, author of
Scrum Shortcuts Without Cutting Corners

"In a field where frameworks and methodologies get much of the attention, it's refreshing to read a story from the trenches about the power of culture. Can it be created, cultivated, and scaled beyond the team? The evidence presented here indicates that it's possible even in challenging circumstances and when the concept is new to everyone. With plenty of examples to show the way, this is a great source of ideas and inspiration for anyone looking to create a sense of common purpose for a group of teams."

- Brian Adkins, Principal Agile Consultant

"This is a brilliant book! It combines relatable examples with actionable outcomes to make it a very engaging read. Anyone looking for ways to improve team performance would benefit from reading it."

- Jackie Grills, Chief Financial Officer

In memory of my friend Jean Tabaka
1954-2016
***

Acknowledgements

There are so many people without whom this book would not have been possible.

My partner, Kylie, for, as you would say, giving me a two-year leave pass and sending me to book camp.

My parents Ros & David McCarthy and Harold & Krystyna Campbell-Pretty for always believing in me. And my brother Josh because he wanted to be in the book! ;-)

Mark Richards, my friend and business partner. This all started with you. Thank you so much for your support and friendship and the countless hours you have spent editing my blogs and presentations.

The EDW Agile Release Train—what can I say? You have been the inspiration for my work and this book. What an amazing ride with a phenomenal group of people.

Team Loco: Megan "Megsie" Anderson, Wayne "Wayno" Palmer, Julian "Smurf" Senanthi-Raja, Amol "DJ Amol" Narayan, Teresa "T-Bone" Simmermacher. Thank you for keeping me sane and making my Agile Release Train dream a reality.

The crew at Context Matters—quite simply, you rock!

Karina Woolmer—thank you for introducing me to Dave Thompson. All I had to say was I wanted to write a book and you connected me with THE guy who could help me make it happen.

Dave Thompson, Matt Gardner, and Ben Reeves from the Inspirational Book Writers Retreat—thank you for creating such an amazing space for me to focus in, knuckle down, and get this done!

Gene Kim and Steve Farber—thank you both so much for stepping up and filling Jean's shoes in writing my foreword. I can't think of two better people to represent her.

The folks on all the Agile Release Trains I have had the pleasure of working with—thank you for letting me be a part of your world and for letting me share your stories.

The reviewers: Mark Richards, Andy Kelk, Even Leybourn, Sandy Mamoli, Ilan Goldstein, Brain Adkins, Ken Collier, Anders Ivarsson and Jackie Grills—thank you for taking time out of your busy schedules to provide me with constructive feedback and additional thoughts. This book is better because of you.

Table of Contents

Foreword by Steve Farber

It always amazes me how quickly we business people latch on to new buzzwords and catchphrases—and I've been around long enough to see some of the classics come and go.

Remember TQM and the Quality Circles that came along with it? How about Re-Engineering? And when Smith and Katzenbach wrote *The Wisdom of Teams* back in 1993, "Teamwork" stormed the business-speak world with a vengeance.

Overnight, it seemed, teams were everything. As a result, we started calling every collection of human beings a "team"—even when they weren't. *Especially* when they weren't.

But it made us feel cutting-edge, hip, up to date with the latest, hot-stuff business practices.

But calling something a team and behaving like a team are entirely different things, and the practice of "teaming" changes significantly depending on the context.

I remember hearing the venerable Peter Drucker lamenting at an HR conference (circa 1994) about the rampant, loose usage of the T word. "A team is not a team is not a team," he said. "A baseball team is fundamentally different from a rugby team. A rugby team has little in common with an HR team. We need to stop using the word to describe everything. There's more than one kind of team."

Then, a decade or so later, along came the word "Tribe," and here you are reading a book called, *Tribal Unity: Getting from Teams to Tribes by Creating a One Team Culture.*

Let me be clear: I'm not a cynic. I may be the furthest thing from it, truth be told. I'm not saying the words "Team" and "Tribe" (and all the popular biz-jargon) are to be scoffed at and dismissed.

Quite the opposite, in fact: the reason these words became popular to begin with is because we know they're important, critical practices that we should all embrace—often times because we experience an all-too-painful shortage of them.

I *am* saying that using the words is not enough. Calling your folks a Tribe or a Team does not make it so—action does, behavior does. And action and behavior require the right kind of knowledge.

And that's where this great book comes in.

Em Campbell-Pretty has taken the mystery out of tribe and team dynamics. She lays out the particulars—the questions, processes, guidelines, and examples—that you can use right now to solve problems, create new products, and change the world by acting as a team, by being part of a tribe.

No matter what you call yourself.

Steve Farber
Author, *The Radical Leap, The Radical Edge, Greater Than Yourself*
San Diego, CA

Foreword by Gene Kim

Be forewarned: by writing this book, Em Campbell-Pretty is fully showcasing her intelligence, intuition, and even cunning nature. But thank goodness, because this is what our industry needs:

Bureaucratic, command and control processes have dominated how large, complex organizations have operated for nearly a century — however, many of our common experiences show that this type of leadership is becoming increasingly ill-suited for complex work we do in technology, where small accidents can cause catastrophic failures, and where we also need to create creating dynamic, learning organizations that continually reinforce high-trust cultural norms, so that we can innovate and win in the marketplace.

However, we may glibly say that the days of command and control leadership may be coming to an end, it is far more difficult to crisply articulate what to replace it with.

Em Campbell-Pretty provides a glimpse into the future of what this reality looks like: she starts by sharing the beginning of her own journey in 2009 as the business sponsor of a strategic $200+ million Enterprise Data Warehouse initiative that puts her into a technology leadership role.

In the adventure that follows, the Agile principles are among the least radical that she embraces and deploys to create high-performing technology teams. The craftiness of this book is that the reader will likely enthusiastically agree that these management practices not only make sense, but are things we should put into practice right away.

The bodies of knowledge that she pulls together to arm technology leaders is breathtaking and impressive, covering Agile, kanban, organizational change management, and gemba walks, to the role of tribe building, embracing vulnerability and self-organizing teams, servant leadership and other techniques that deserve to become more mainstream.

I heartily recommend this book to anyone who wants a glimpse of what technology leaders should be doing to help create world-class technology organisations.

Gene Kim
Co-author of *The Phoenix Project* (2013) and *DevOps Handbook* (2016)
Portland, OR

Preface

I don't assume what worked for me will work for you, but I do want to inspire you as you contemplate what an intentional culture of joy could look like in your world—Richard Sheridan, *Joy, Inc.*

This book is for everyone who aspires to make their workplace "a great place to work". One of my inspirations for this book was Richard Sheridan's *Joy, Inc.* It is the story of Sheridan's company Menlo Innovations and their culture of joy. *Joy Inc.* inspired me on two fronts: the first being the idea of a business book based on a true story to provide "tangible examples" that "can be very helpful" but "are rare in business books."[1] Secondly, and most significantly, Menlo's "intentional culture of joy" perfectly mirrors my beliefs about the importance of creating great places to work. It is this sentiment of "an intentional culture of joy" that lies at the heart of *Tribal Unity*.

Like Sheridan, my story starts in the world of software development; however, unlike Sheridan, I did not grow up in this world. As a business person working in large enterprises, my experience with software development teams was anything but joyful until I found the world of Agile. This is not a book about Agile per se, but it does borrow many practices from the world of Agile.

For those not familiar with the Agile, it is an umbrella term for a number of "lightweight" software development methodologies that were developed in the 1990s. Many of them, like Scrum, are still very popular today. In 2001, seventeen thought leaders in the world of "lightweight" software development gathered for a weekend at the Snow-

---

[1] Richard Sheridan, *Joy, Inc.: How We Built a Workplace People Love*, (New York: Penguin, 2013), Kindle Edition, location 218.

bird ski resort in Utah. The aim of the gathering was to identify areas of commonality across their methodologies. The result was the Agile Manifesto.[2]

Manifesto for Agile Software Development

We are uncovering better ways of developing
software by doing it and helping others do it.
Through this work we have come to value:

Individuals and interactions over processes and tools
Working software over comprehensive documentation
Customer collaboration over contract negotiation
Responding to change over following a plan

That is, while there is value in the items on
the right, we value the items on the left more.

Kent Beck	James Grenning	Robert C. Martin
Mike Beedle	Jim Highsmith	Steve Mellor
Arie van Bennekum	Andrew Hunt	Ken Schwaber
Alistair Cockburn	Ron Jeffries	Jeff Sutherland
Ward Cunningham	Jon Kern	Dave Thomas
Martin Fowler	Brian Marick	

---

[2] "Manifesto for Agile Software Development", accessed August 26, 2016, http://agilemanifesto.org/

Principles behind the Agile Manifesto

We follow these principles:

Our highest priority is to satisfy the customer
through early and continuous delivery
of valuable software.

Welcome changing requirements, even late in
development. Agile processes harness change for
the customer's competitive advantage.

Deliver working software frequently, from a
couple of weeks to a couple of months, with a
preference to the shorter timescale.

Business people and developers must work
together daily throughout the project.

Build projects around motivated individuals.
Give them the environment and support they need,
and trust them to get the job done.

The most efficient and effective method of
conveying information to and within a development
team is face-to-face conversation.

Working software is the primary measure of progress.

Agile processes promote sustainable development.
The sponsors, developers, and users should be able
to maintain a constant pace indefinitely.

Continuous attention to technical excellence
and good design enhances agility.

Simplicity--the art of maximizing the amount
of work not done--is essential.

The best architectures, requirements, and designs
emerge from self-organizing teams.

At regular intervals, the team reflects on how
to become more effective, then tunes and adjusts
its behavior accordingly.

While Agile started life in the world of software development, it has increasingly become part of many kinds of businesses. For example, there is Agile Marketing, Agile Human Resources, and Agile Contact Centres. I have even worked with an Agile Enterprise Portfolio Management Office. It is the underlying premise of this book that the tools and techniques contained within are equally, if not more, applicable outside the world of software development.

The main case study that runs through this book relates to what I fondly refer to as the EDW tribe. It was working with this group of people where I first experienced many of the practices contained in *Tribal Unity*. It is probably worth noting that while the book mainly talks about the patterns that I have found to be both successful and repeatable, there were many, many experiments along the way that led to us discovering and settling on these techniques.

My Story

My first foray into Agile was as the business sponsor of a $200-million-dollar program of work to build out an Enterprise Data Warehouse (EDW).[3] I had spent almost a year shopping an EDW "enhancement" program around the company, including getting to pitch it in person to the CEO. For the six months following the CEO's endorsement of the program, we were in a holding pattern. The funding, whilst agreed, would not become available until July 1, so the decision was made to pass to me the business ownership of a related but much smaller program that was already in flight.

This program had a long and chequered history; it had already been in progress for three years. I had actually been involved in its inception as a subject matter expert and key contributor to the feasibility, before I moved on to another role. In the meantime, the program had spent 12 months interviewing 144 people across the enterprise and compiling a 200-page requirements document.

It took another year for the program to get its business case approved. It was like a comedy of errors. The technology folks had been given the requirements and asked to provide an architectural solution and a time-and-cost estimate for delivery. They went away for a few months and came back with a large bill and long timeline, only to receive the feedback that their solution was not "strategic enough". So the process

---

[3] Right now I can see you asking yourself, what is a Data Warehouse? Don't worry, I've been there! The first time I encountered a Data Warehouse was the day I started a job where apparently I "owned" one! As an ex-market researcher and call centre manager, I was completely lost. The simplest way to think of a Data Warehouse is like a library for all your organisation's data. The good news is you don't need to know anything about Data Warehousing to read this book!

was repeated and a more strategic solution was identified, and the cost went up and the delivery timeline extended.

Eventually, everyone involved decided to cut their losses and agreed to focus in on the scope that could be delivered in the 10 remaining months of the financial year. This turned out to be 10 work packages, which was about a third of the total scope. If you have 10 work packages to deliver in 10 months, obviously the last thing to do would be to start all 10 at once! But that is exactly what they did!

For the next three months, the program team ran workshops all day every day with the business stakeholders. From these workshops emerged another 400 pages of documentation. The next challenge was getting the business to sign off on the documents, so that another document could be produced! This was the moment when I arrived back on the scene.

I was immediately injected into the daily status call. The clock was ticking and the program was in crisis mode. Not a single line of code had been written and there were only five months left for these first 10 work packages to be delivered. The calls were focused on getting document sign-off. The technology team was eager to have signed-off requirements to feed in to the "SRS". My first question—what was an SRS and why was it so important? I learnt that SRS stood for System Requirements Specification and that this was the document we would send to the offshore team so they knew what to build. I figured it must be important then and did what I could to help the technology team to get sign-off.

By the end of the 10 months, one of the 10 work packages was deployed to production. It then spent six months in User Acceptance Testing. Suffice to say I was VERY concerned about the ability of this team to deliver my three-year strategic program of work that was close to 10 times the size of this program.

It was at this moment that I started to explore the idea of Agile.

At the time my knowledge of Agile was sketchy. I can remember a program manager having explained Scrum to me a year or two back. I swear she said that we would create a project team that we would lock in a room for 30 days and at the end of this period called a "Sprint" they would emerge with working solutions. It sounded very strange but also magical![4]

Not feeling at all confident about this Scrum and Sprint business, I went to the font of all knowledge—the Amazon online bookstore—and started shopping! I read Craig Larman's *Agile and Iterative Development: A Manager's Guide* and Ralph Hughes' *Agile Data Warehousing*. I was now armed and dangerous! I recall one of my first "bright ideas" derived from this was to inflict daily stand-ups meeting on the program team. It still makes me cringe to think of these daily status meetings full of project managers and an Excel spreadsheet full of actions.

While I didn't make things any better, I'm not sure I made them any worse, but clearly the IT establishment was unhappy, as it was not long before a bus full of highly paid consultants landed on my doorstep, peddling a custom-built Agile process for our very special and unique circumstances. It was only a matter of months before I found myself the not-so-proud owner of a 70-page Agile process for Enterprise Data Warehousing.

---

[4] Scrum is the world's most widely used agile method. The roles, events, artifacts and rules of Scrum can be found in the The Scrum Guide™.
A Sprint (also called an iteration) is a short time box in which a team works on a committed backlog of work. Most Agile teams use two-week Sprints, but they can be as short as a week or as long a month. See: http://www.scrumguides.org/scrum-guide.html

In the meantime, there had been a CIO mandate to go Agile. The organisation had chosen 10 strategic programs to start with but my program was not one of them. Despite our domain being "out of scope" some of the IT crew managed to enrol themselves in Agile Fundamentals training, but they did not invite their business counterparts. There was uproar. Well, okay, I created the uproar, but it was ridiculous: on one hand I was footing the bill for a custom Agile process for Enterprise Data Warehousing; on the other hand, the people who actually did the work were off on Agile Fundamentals training that one would assume was probably not consistent with our new customised Agile process.

So I took my concerns to the director in charge of the domain and he directed his program manager to "talk to the Agile people" about getting everyone through the new corporate Agile Fundamentals training. Later I would learn he had an incentive. Every IT director had a target to deliver 10% of their domain's projects using Agile as the delivery methodology and the director in charge of the Data Warehousing domain had not yet met his target. And so my real journey into Agile and Lean had begun.[5]

Both my team and the IT leadership team went on the two-day "Agile Fundamentals" course. It was here that I first met Mark Richards, the Agile coach and trainer who would in due course be instrumental in helping me achieve Tribal Unity.

---

[5] Lean is the term the Western world uses to describe the Toyota Production System (TPS). It became known as Lean in the early 1990s as a result of James Womack's book *The Machine That Changed the World*. Taiichi Ohno, the father of TPS, described the process as follows: *"All we are doing is looking at the time line, from the moment the customer gives us an order to the point when we collect the cash. And we are reducing the time line by reducing the non-value adding wastes."*

Inspired by our two days of training, we went about setting up our first Agile team. It was half onshore and half offshore and didn't include a single person who had ever done anything Agile before. It really was a very bizarre choice. However, this team delivered. Well, sort of delivered; at least they delivered faster than any team in this domain had done before. It took three or four months but we did get some "working" software, for a given definition of working!

Despite the numerous technical challenges that surrounded this first release, the team's small success inspired us to spin up more and more Agile teams. Within six months we had six Agile teams across four projects, doing what I like to call "the worst Agile known to man". Surprisingly this was an improvement on the previous approach, although still not a sustainable model.

And then everything changed. There was a restructure. A complete "spill and fill" of the general managers in my group. A new role was created to lead the technology team responsible for the Enterprise Data Warehouse. A nationwide search was conducted to find someone to fill the position, but they were unable to secure a suitable candidate.[6] Personally, I chose to apply for the job that looked most like my existing job. I didn't get it. I was devastated.

My manager suggested that I consider taking on the vacant EDW GM role. I was not at all convinced that this was a good idea. After all, I was in no way qualified for this gig. I was a business person. I had always been a business person. When I joined the company, my team had to explain to me what a Data Warehouse was. This was utter madness.

And then it dawned on me: what an opportunity!

---

[6] I have a theory that anyone qualified had heard stories of this EDW and quite simply was not stupid enough to apply.

I had just returned from my summer holiday in Bali, where I had been reading Dean Leffingwell's *Scaling Software Agility*. One of the core concepts in this book was the idea of an Agile Release Train: a team of Agile teams.[7] I really liked the idea, but as a business person I could not tell the technology folk that they needed to try it; however, if I was a business person leading a technology team, there would be no one to stop me! Now, this was appealing. Coupled with the advice of my lieutenant, who quite rightly pointed out that as a business person with no IT qualifications I was NEVER going to be handed an opportunity like this again, I was sold.

Over the next two years I would lead the transformation of the worst IT team in the company, whose culture was universally described as toxic by anyone who came in contact with it, into a leading example of a great culture on a global stage. We would do this through the creation of the EDW Agile Release Train. We went from a situation where we could not hire people in the local job market because our reputation was so bad, to a world in which people were queuing to come and join the tribe.

It was the story of the EDW Agile Release Train that led to me being invited to give my first presentation at an Agile conference. It was at this conference that I first realised there was something a little bit special about my story. It was day two and Mark and I were sitting at the front of the room for the morning keynote. (Mark hates it but I always make him sit up the front because I can't see from down the back!) There were just the two of us at the table when Jean Tabaka came over and asked if she could join us. (For those who have not heard of Jean, she was an Agile thought leader and author of *Collaboration Explained* which meant she had celebrity status at Agile conferences.) We were all listening to Drew Jemilo and Rachel Weston Rowell talking about Agile

---

[7] Dean Leffingwell, *Scaling Software Agility: Best Practices for Large Enterprises*, (Boston: Pearson, 2007), Kindle Edition.

Release Trains when Drew described the train as a self-organising team of teams. I heard Jean mutter to herself "That's not how _____ does it." Never one to pass up an opportunity, I leant over and whispered "that is how we do it."

Well, that got Jean's attention. I started to tell her about the approach I had taken with EDW Agile Release Train, in particular our focus on what I called "scaling culture". I invited her to attend our talk so that she could learn more about it but she had a client meeting at that time. She told me I needed to run an open space session on scaling culture. I recall squirming with discomfort. I had never run an open space session before. I messaged Mark: *Jean says we should do an open space on scaling culture. Will you help me?* [8]

Sure, he said.

The next afternoon a small group of people gathered to hear what Mark and I had to say about scaling culture and Jean turned up and took notes! We were so chuffed![9] We learned that Jean was heading to Australia in three weeks' time and would be spending a week in Melbourne, so we invited her to visit the EDW Agile Release Train and see it for herself. Her feedback— "Well, you sure didn't oversell it!" She went on to comment on how open the team was to different experiences and asked how we went about creating an environment where traditionally introverted software engineers from a diverse range of cultures and backgrounds were so willing to participate in team activities.

---

[8] Open space is an approach to hosting meetings and conferences. The approach is most distinctive for its initial lack of an agenda, which sets the stage for the meeting's participants to create the agenda for themselves in the first 30 – 90 minutes of the meeting or event. (Wikipedia, accessed August 26, 2016, https://en.wikipedia.org/wiki/Open_Space_Technology)

[9] This is Aussie for "very pleased".

Jean and I stayed in touch over the following six months. From time to time I would send her amusing anecdotes of the goings-on with the EDW train. Somewhere along the way we decided to co-present on scaling culture at Agile 2014.[10] As we brainstormed our proposal, I started to tell Jean about a conversation I had been having with one of my team. He had made the observation that the train had become like a tribe. Jean loved it. The theme for our talk became Creating Agile Tribes.

© 2016 Lynne Cazaly Image used with permission. lynnecazaly.com

Which brings us to today. Over three years since I started talking about scaling culture and creating Agile tribes, it would seem I have found my calling. I left the EDW tribe over two years ago. Since then I have been working with teams of teams, applying what I have learned about scaling culture and creating tribes. Through this work I have identified a number of repeatable patterns and practices that have been used both within and outside IT to transform the culture of organisations, creating Tribal Unity.

---

[10] The Agile 20xx conference series is the world's largest Agile conference.

Introduction

Birds flock, fish swim, people "tribe"—David Logan, *Tribal Leadership*.

Since the beginning of time humans have formed tribes, it is just what we do. Many associate tribes with Dunbar's number—the number of people that humans are best able to maintain stable relationships with. This is generally considered to fall in the range of 100 to 250 people, with 150 being most common. In *Tribal Leadership* David Logan suggests that once a group grows to over 150 it will naturally split in two.[11] This number turns up time and again throughout human history: nomadic tribes, Amish communities and military units among others. It is also the maximum number of people in an Agile Release Train (according to the Scaled Agile Framework)[12] and the maximum number of people in a tribe in Spotify's Agile "model".[13]

Going beyond the raw numbers, my favourite definition of a tribe comes from marketing guru and author Seth Godin: *"A tribe is a group of people connected to one another, connected to a leader, and connected to an idea."*[14] It is this definition that underpins my approach to creating Tribal Unity.

---

[11] David Logan, John King and Halee Fischer-Wright, *Tribal Leadership: How Successful Groups form Great Organizations*, (HarperCollins, 2008), Kindle Edition, location 114.

[12] The Scaled Agile Framework or SAFe is an approach for applying Agile, which was historically used by small teams, to teams of hundreds or even thousands. For more information see: http://scaledagileframework.com/

[13] Henrik Kniberg and Anders Ivarsson, *Scaling Agile @ Spotify: with Tribes, Squads, Chapters & Guilds*, 2012, accessed 26 August, 2016, https://ucvox.files.wordpress.com/2012/11/113617905-scaling-agile-spotify-11.pdf

[14] Seth Godin, *Tribes: We Need You to Lead Us*, (London: Hachette Digital, 2008), Kindle Edition, location 36.

So, if tribes form naturally, what is the big deal? Well, not all tribes are created equal. Logan suggests that: "What makes some tribes more effective than others is culture."[15] His book is the result of 10 years of field research, across 24,000 people in 24 different organisations. Logan and his team identified five stages of tribal culture, that can be recognised by the language that they use when they talk about themselves.

The five stages are:

Stage 1 – This is the culture of street gangs and prisons. Their language is "Life sucks". They make up approximately 2% of professionals in the U.S.

Stage 2 – This is the culture that we see when we watch *The Office*. A culture that many might associate with the public service. Their language is "My life sucks". This culture is estimated to be present in 25% of U.S. workplaces.

Stage 3 – This is the most prevalent culture in U.S. workplaces, being found in about 49% of them. Their language is "I am great and you are not". This is a culture often associated with doctors, lawyers, and sales people.

Stage 4 – This stage is where "everyone seems happy, inspired, and genuine". It occurs in about 22% of U.S. workplaces. Their language is "We are great, they are not!" This is often the culture of sporting teams; just think of all those great sporting club rivalries.

Stage 5 –While it is not considered sustainable, great organisations have "bursts" of stage 5. Their language is "Life is great!". This is the culture of history-making teams like the teams that win Olympic gold medals or the team behind the original Apple Macintosh. This only occurs in about 2% of U.S. workplaces.

---

[15] David Logan, *Tribal Leadership*, location 499.

So how do we create great tribes that people want to be a part of?

One way is to read David Logan's book, which I highly recommend. The crux of Logan's approach is to focus in on the language and behaviour of the organisation. In essence, the leader needs to listen to the language, identify the stage, and then "upgrade" the tribe to the next level using specific "leverage points".

You could also continue reading this book, which I hope you do!

My approach is a little different to Logan's. It is based on experience rather than research. I also focus in on teams of teams and tribes, rather than taking a whole-of-organisation view. The book is intended as a practical guide for leaders and tribe members on how to effectively improve the culture of their tribe.

This book is broken into six sections:
Part 1 – Creating Great Teams
Part 2 – Connecting Teams and Creating Tribes
Part 3 – Connecting to a Leader
Part 4 – Connecting to an Idea
Part 5 – Sustaining Tribal Unity
Part 6 – Engaging Management in Tribal Unity

Those from the Agile community may decide to skip Part 1; however, it is a light and potentially entertaining read as long as you are aware that I am not trying to "tell you how to suck eggs".[16]

---

[16] "English language saying meaning that a person is giving advice to someone else about a subject of which they are already familiar (and probably more so than the first person)." Wikipedia, *Teaching grandmother to suck eggs*, accessed September 10, 2016, https://en.wikipedia.org/wiki/Teaching_grandmother_to_suck_eggs

Part 6 is intended to answer the question, how do I get my management to engage in all this Tribal Unity "mumbo jumbo"? While it was written with the intent of helping those on the front line, coaches and managers may well find this content useful. I will leave you to decide for yourself if this is for you.

Those using SAFe, or thinking about using SAFe, should think of the tribe as another term for an Agile Release Train. Every practice I advocate in this book has been tried and tested with real-world Agile Release Trains; three of these are official SAFe case studies that you can read about on the Scaled Agile Framework website[17,18,19]

---

[17] See: http://scaledagileframework.com/telstra/

[18] See: http://scaledagileframework.com/rmit/

[19] See: http://scaledagileframework.com/westpac-case-study/

PART 1

CREATING GREAT TEAMS

... create a team that acts as a team, one in which the members support one another and work together to achieve the results you need
—Christine Comaford, *Smart Tribes*.

The foundations of an effective tribe are effective teams. Therefore, the first step in building your tribe is to create great teams: specifically, teams of seven people ± two with a shared mission. Both the size and the mission are important.

Let's start with size. Seven people ± two is the common rule of thumb of the Agile movement when it comes to team size. Some people accept this and work to this as a rule; others ignore it at their peril. Quite simply, the problem with large teams is that they struggle to communicate. For example, if you have a team of three people, there are three lines of communication, so that works pretty well. If you have a team of five people, there are 10 different lines of communication. That is also manageable. But when you have a team of 10 people it is a whole

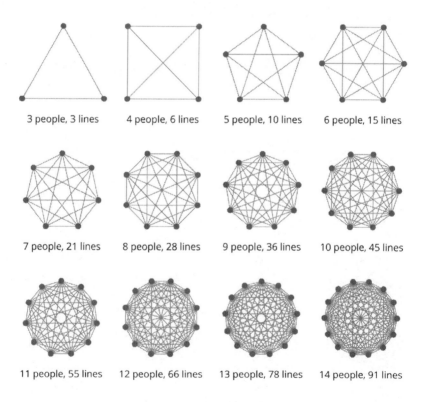

| 3 people, 3 lines | 4 people, 6 lines | 5 people, 10 lines | 6 people, 15 lines |

| 7 people, 21 lines | 8 people, 28 lines | 9 people, 36 lines | 10 people, 45 lines |

| 11 people, 55 lines | 12 people, 66 lines | 13 people, 78 lines | 14 people, 91 lines |

different story! A team of 10 people has 45 different lines of communication and that makes it really, really hard to keep everyone aligned. Plus, in most organisations there will be other people outside the team that the team interacts with regularly, maybe a customer, or a project manager, or a supplier. All of these people just add to the complexity.

This is a lesson I learned the hard way: not once, but twice in my career. The first time was on one of the teams involved in the "worst Agile known to man" period of my career. I was still in the role of business sponsor at this time. One of the projects in the program had made a request for additional funding. They had been in-flight for about four months and so far all they had delivered was a baby boy called Dax.[20]

Putting the lack of delivery aside, this request for additional funding was problematic for me, as I was getting a lot of pressure from the organisation to cut costs. I was telling my coach, Mark Richards, about my woes when he suggested reducing the size of the teams. He said I could probably afford to halve the team size without suffering a reduction in throughput. It sounded too good to be true, but given the lack of options available to me, I decided to give it a go.

Being in "the business", I had no control over team composition, but I did control the budget. So I told the IT program manager that I was halving his budget, in order to force his hand and reduce the team size. It would be fair to say he was not happy! However, an interesting side effect of this ask was it resulted in us having to work out who was actually on the project team. We found 23 people!

The program manager came back to me with three options: 1) leave things as they were; 2) make a slight reduction in team size and keep to the committed delivery schedule; or 3) cut the team in half (as per

---

[20] Although I'm not sure anyone other than the scrum master (whose son it was) contributed much to that delivery!

the revised budget) and deliver less scope. I chose option 3. This did not go down well at all. Apparently if a consultant gives you a proposal with three options you are supposed to pick the middle one. Who knew?! He told me if we went with my solution we were not going to deliver on our commitments. I said that's okay, you have never delivered on your commitment before so I will take the cheap option!

The team size was halved and in the next two-week time box, their throughput remained constant and in the following two weeks the throughput went up! We went on to "right-size" all the Agile teams on the program, eventually landing on a standard team size of eight people.

Of course you would think that I would have learned from this—but a year or so later I fell into a similar trap. By this time, I was leading the technology team. We had been having great success with our Agile Release Train, so much so that the demand for our services was far outstripping our capacity to deliver. Remembering that the optimal size of an Agile team was seven ± two, in theory we could add another developer to each team and increase throughput. Genius!

We went about recruiting a new developer for each team. Eight weeks went by and nothing changed. Throughput did not increase. Nor did it decline; it essentially remained constant. It appears Brooks was right: nine women can't make a baby in one month! Having long been an advocate of Brooks' work, it was fascinating to see it materialise in front of me.[21]

We took the data to the teams and asked them what they had observed since the arrival of an additional person in their team. The feedback

---

[21] In *The Mythical Man-Month* Fred Brooks indicates that one should not consider people and time to be interchangeable, using the following metaphor: *"The bearing of a child takes nine months, no matter how many women are assigned."*

was consistent. Team members had become more focused on their areas of specialisation and the team had started to lose the cross-skilling that had been central to our early Agile success. The consensus was that we should return to eight-person teams and consider experimenting with even smaller teams in the future. We did this by spinning off an additional team and of course, this time the throughput went up! My biggest regret from this experiment was not taking the opportunity to try out team self-selection when we reshuffled everyone in order to create the additional team.

Team Self-Selection

What would you do if you weren't afraid?
—Sandy Mamoli and David Mole,
Creating Great Teams: How Self-Selection Lets People Excel.

While the idea of self-selecting teams has been around for a long time, it has more recently become popular in Agile circles thanks to the work of Sandy Mamoli and David Mole, authors of *Creating Great Teams: How Self-Selection Lets People Excel*. Self-selection means letting the people who do the work decide which team they want to be a part of. According to Sandy and David a precondition for a self-selection event is a clear mission and vision for each team.[22] Just think of any sporting team, amateur or professional: the mission and vision is always clear—to win the game! Whether you already have teams or you are looking at creating teams you need to be clear about their missions, then ensure that teams have the right sets of skills to deliver on those missions, ideally autonomously.

---

[22] Sandy Mamoli and David Mole, *Creating Great Teams: How Self-Selection Lets People Excel*, (Raleigh: Pragmatic Bookshelf, 2015), PDF Edition, p21.

I would add to that that we want real teams, not just groups of people who happen to work together. Harvard University Professor J. Richard Hackman defines a "real team" as having: *"a team task, clear boundaries, clearly specified authority to manage their own work processes, and membership stability over some reasonable period of time."*[23] It is this first condition—team task—that is similar to this concept of a shared mission. Hackman uses the example of a string quartet where all members need to contribute for the team to deliver. Sporting teams also tend to fit this model. The second condition is about being clear who is actually on the team. You may laugh, but hopefully the example I just shared of the 23-person team, where we had to actively go out and identify the team members, is a clear illustration that these things are sometimes more difficult than they seem.

Most people find the thought of letting people choose their own teams utterly terrifying. I know I did when I first heard about it. How could the team possibly know how to create the right teams? Surely they couldn't be trusted to create evenly balanced teams. It was all just a little bit too hippie for my taste. Until, as is often the case, I saw how this approach could actually provide a solution to a problem.

These days much of my work is in helping organisations launch Agile Release Trains, teams of Agile teams. One of the first challenges we face when getting ready to launch a train is team design. Often the existing teams are functionally based, which is not ideal when we need real teams with all the skills to deliver on a mission! I would always suggest self-selection, but it was too big a leap of faith for most clients. Never one to be easily dissuaded, I continued to suggest self-selection until I found a willing victim!

---

[23] J. Richard Hackman, *Leading Teams: Setting the Stage for Great Performances,* (Boston: Harvard University Press, 2002), Kindle Edition, location 737.

Running a self-selection event requires a fair amount of logistical fore-thought. In particular, you need to be clear on the missions for the teams and the constraints. Sandy and David advise that you minimise the constraints.[24] From my experiences, I would advocate that while you should minimise constraints you should also be transparent about your expectations. One organisation for which I facilitated a self-selection event had an expectation that a set of evenly sized and skilled teams would be the outcome of the event; however, in an effort to minimise constraints they did not communicate this to the team, resulting a need to reshuffle people after the fact. While this was far from catastrophic it was definitely uncomfortable.

A self-selection event usually takes about half a day. It starts by everyone picking up a prepared photo of themselves when they arrive. The teams are then seeded with a mission and someone who knows about that mission. In Agile this person is often the product owner.[25] Each product or mission owner gets an opportunity to "sell" their mission to the group. The group then goes through three or four rounds of self-selecting into teams and playing back their status until they settle. Each round involves people choosing a team for themselves by placing their photo on one of the team sheets. In the playbacks each team shares with the group if they are under or oversized and what skills they have too many or too little of. This then lays out the problem to solve for the next round of self-selection.

---

[24] Sandy and David only use three constraints:
1. Teams have to be capable of delivering end to end.
2. Teams have to be made up of three to seven people.
3. Teams have to be co-located.
Mamoli and Mole, *Creating Great Teams*, p29-30.

[25] The role of a product owner is to maximise the value of the product and the work of the development team. See: http://www.scrumguides.org/scrum-guide.html#team-po.

In line with Hackman's guidance you should expect the team's membership to be stable "over some reasonable period of time". Sandy and David suggest revisiting the self-selection after six months so that the people participating in the event know that they are not stuck with their choices for life.

If you want to understand more about the nuts and bolts of doing a self-selection event, there is no better place to start than Sandy and David's book. They provide a step-by-step guide on what you need to do to succeed, answers to frequently asked questions, suggestions on how to respond to concerns from management and participants, and a handy set of checklists to keep you on track.

Of course it is not mandatory to use self-selection, but if your goal is to improve the culture of your organisation and make it a truly great place to work, then I can't imagine a better place to start. You may also like to consider Hackman's estimation that 30% of a team's performance is determined by "how the initial launch of the team goes."[26]

Should self-selection not be your cup of tea you can take a less radical approach to team design. In these scenarios my default approach is to write the names of every person in the organisation and their specialisation on an index card, decide the constraints and missions for the teams, then work with the leadership team to fill out the teams using the index cards. Using physical cards helps make the process more interactive and inclusive of everyone's view. Don't be surprised if you have too many or not enough people to fill your teams. This is likely to happen especially if the team's boundaries are not clear. Remember that surfacing the existing problems with the organisation's skill mix is the first step to solving them.

---

[26] J. Richard Hackman, *Collaborative Intelligence: Using Teams to Solve Hard Problems*, (San Francisco: Berrett-Koehler, 2011), Kindle Edition, location 2612.

Team Work Practices

This leaves just one of Hackman's team conditions to be addressed: *clearly specified authority to manage their own work processes*. This does not mean the team has to have complete autonomy, but they do need clarity on where the boundaries lie. Ideally, determining the boundaries is a collaborative process. Author Jurgen Appelo has a great tool for facilitating a discussion like this called Delegation Poker.[27] It uses the "seven levels of delegation" to provide a range of levels of empowerment in contrast to the more traditional binary view.

Seven Levels of Delegation

Level 1: Tell: You make decisions and announce them to your people.

Level 2: Sell: You make decisions, but you attempt to gain commitment from workers by "selling" your idea to them.

Level 3: Consult: You invite and weigh input from workers before coming to a decision. But you make it clear that it's you who is making the decisions.

Level 4: Agree: You invite workers to join in a discussion and to reach consensus as a group. Your voice is equal to the others.

Level 5: Advise: You attempt to influence workers by telling them what your opinion is, but ultimately you leave it up to them to decide.

---

[27] You can download Delegation Poker free of charge at: m30.me/delegation-poker

Level 6: Inquire: You let the team decide first, with the suggestion that it would be nice, though not strictly necessary, if they can convince you afterward.

Level 7: Delegate: You leave it entirely up to the team to deal with the matter while you go out and have a good time (or use that time to manage the system).[28]

If I was to offer a recommendation it would be to consider the minimal level of agility you expect from these teams and make this the only constraint you place on their work practices. I use the term agility loosely, as I don't think it is necessary for all teams to be Agile per se, but I do think there are a number of Agile practices that have close to universal applicability. I refer to this as Minimal Viable Agility and include practices such as cadence-based retrospectives, visualisation, and daily stand-ups.[29]

Inspect and Adapt on Cadence

*Retrospectives enable whole-team learning, act as catalysts for
change, and generate action*
—Esther Derby and Diana Larson,
Agile Retrospectives: Making Good Teams Great.

If you have to choose just one practice for your teams to adopt, this is the one. Inspecting and adapting on cadence is how you begin to

---

[28] Jurgen Appelo, *Management 3.0: Leading Agile Developers, Developing Agile Leaders,* (Boston: Pearson, 2011), PDF Edition, p127-8.

[29] Whilst Minimal Viable Agility (as I have defined it) does not include technical practices, if you are working with software development teams, Minimal Viable Agility must include clean coding practices.

build a continuous improvement culture. The Agile folks like to call this ritual a retrospective. The idea is that the teams take an hour out on a regular basis, maybe once a fortnight or once a month, and reflect on the way they are working together and how they might improve. Teams are encouraged to choose just one or two improvement items to action before the next retrospective. Over time all these small improvements add up resulting in really high-performing teams.

A very basic retrospective involves three questions, some Post-it notes and Sharpies, some writing, a discussion, and a dot voting exercise to decide on the one or two highest priority actions. The questions might be something like:

- What went well?
- What did not go well?
- What can we do better next time?

While this works, it will get really boring really quickly! My advice is to buy each team a copy of *Agile Retrospectives: Making Good Teams Great* by Esther Derby and Diana Larson. Don't worry, you don't have to be "doing Agile" to get value out of the book and help your teams run fruitful retrospectives.

Visualisation

> *... make all necessary information visible when people need it,*
> *enabling effective collaboration and improvement through*
> *understanding how the work works*
> —Marcus Hammarberg and Joakim Sundén,
> *Kanban in Action.*

One of the best ways I know of to help a team behave like a team is to surface all their work on a physical board. In the Agile world, these boards are often referred to as kanban boards. Kanban is a Japanese term that roughly translates to "signal card". The concept originally comes from the Toyota Production System.

Many boards start out as Post-its with work items written on them stuck on a wall, split into columns that represent the process the work flows through.[30] In most cases just the act of getting the work off spreadsheets or out of the project management tools and making it visible on a wall starts to improve the effectiveness of the team. Teams who visualise their work are better at collaborating. When the team members can all see what each other is working on, they identify duplicated effort and opportunities to help each other. The bottom line is they have a better understanding of their world and how each team member contributes.

You may have noticed that I have made a specific point about physical walls over using digital boards. This is not to imply you should not use tooling; in fact, tooling can also be very powerful, especially when it comes to metrics, which are key to helping you understand and improve your process flow. But digital boards aren't great information radiators. *"An information radiator displays information in a place where passersby can see it. With information radiators, the passersby don't need to ask questions; the information simply hits them as they pass."*[31]

Another advantage of using visualisations like kanban boards is the insights such boards provide into the level of work in process. Kanban practitioners refer to this as WIP. One of the ways that kanban teams improve flow is by limiting WIP, that is putting an explicit cap on the number of tasks the team is working on at any one time. Limiting WIP

---

[30] Marcus Hammarberg and Joakim Sundén, *Kanban in Action,* (New York: Manning, 2014), PDF Edition, chapter 1.

[31] Alistair Cockburn, *Agile Software Development: The Cooperative Game,* (Boston: Pearson, 2007), Kindle Edition, location 3263.

helps reduce the impact of task switching as it forces the team to focus on completing one task before starting another. WIP limits can also help teams identify opportunities to help each other and cross skill as they focus on flowing work across the board.[32]

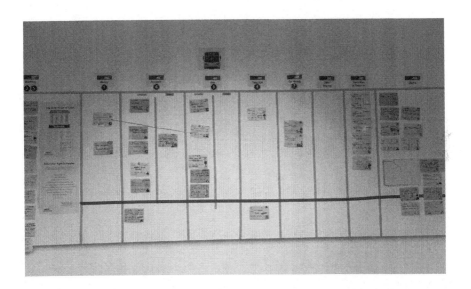

Kanban is one of the most accessible Agile methods to those working outside the software industry; let's face it, it didn't even come from software in the first place. The best resource for understanding the mechanics of a true kanban system is *Kanban in Action* by Marcus Hammarberg and Joakim Sundén. This plain-English, practical explanation of kanban is a must-read for those wanting to get better at using visualisation to meaningfully manage the flow of work through their team.

---

[32] In *Why Software Gets in Trouble*, Gerald M. Weinberg suggests that a team or person splitting their effort across three tasks will only spend 20% of their time on each task with 40% of the total time being lost due to cost of context switching.

Remember kanban is a learning process and the best way to learn is to do. So head to your local hardware store, buy some bright-coloured painter's tape and get going on building your first wall. Use it for a while and when you see the opportunity to make it better tear it down and start again. If nothing else, I can promise you it will be fun!

Daily Communication

The key is to focus on only enough information sharing to solicit requests from parties who need something and promises from parties who will fill the need
—Christine Comaford, *Smart Tribes.*

Once the team can see their work they should be encouraged to communicate a least once a day. You might be familiar with the idea of a daily stand-up commonly used by Agile teams. These meetings are intended as a 15-minute standing meeting. We encourage standing to keep them short. The purpose is to share enough information to solicit requests and receive promises that help the work get done, in service of the team's mission.

It is important to note, the daily stand-up is not a status report. It is an alignment and prioritisation meeting. One of the complaints I often encounter about daily stand-ups is that it is just a status report as the "team" has no shared tasks. Of course, we now know that the problem is likely to be that the team is not a team at all, just a group of people who happen to work together.

The Scrum folk like to use a standard three-question format for their daily stand-ups:
- What did you do yesterday?
- What are you going to do today?
- Do you have any blockers?

This works, but I can also see how this leads to status reporting. Another approach used by my friend Brian Adkins is to ask: "What is our plan of attack—as a team—for our work today?" In his blog post, "Taking the Status Out of Standups",[33] my colleague Mark Richards suggests team members talking to the work items on the wall is another way to mix things up.

[33] Mark Richards, "Taking the Status Out of Standups", *Agile not Anarchy*, April 3, 2015, http://www.agilenotanarchy.com/2015/04/taking-status-out-of-standups.html

Launching Teams

Do you have mechanisms for making decisions,
sharing information, and resolving conflicts so that
clear expectations are set for team behaviours?
—Mario Moussa, *Committed Teams.*

Team agreements, team charters, or social contracts established early in the team's life help the team manage expectations of each other and navigate conflict as it inevitably occurs. The format is less important than having the conversation, making sure everyone is heard, recording the agreement, and then holding each other to account. I like to suggest to teams that they make these agreements visible in their team space. Of course the agreements should not stay static, they should be revisited and evolve over time as the team learns and grows.

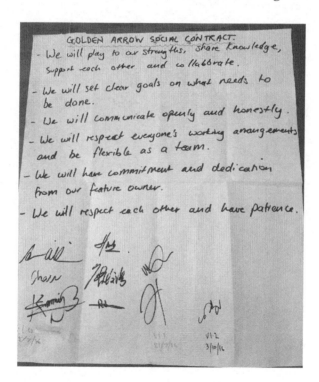

In *Committed Teams*, Mario Moussa et al. suggest using the following four questions to seed the discussion about team norms:
- How will we handle conflict?
- How will we communicate?
- How will we make decisions?
- Have we focused on just a few rules that matter?[34]

Co-location

Given that complete communication is never possible, the task on a project is not to try for complete communication but to manage the incompleteness of our communications
—Alistair Cockburn, *Agile Software Development.*

When you are creating teams, I recommend considering co-location as a constraint. It is just so hard for teams to bond when they do not spend time together face to face. I know this can be really, really hard in today's distributed working environment and I know that insisting on co-location can be politically awkward, but I can promise you it is worth it. If you cannot co-locate all the teams in your tribe, at least try and co-locate teams rather than having each team spread across multiple locations.

Recently I was working with an organisation that defaults to using distributed teams. A colleague and I were facilitating a very simple and straightforward workshop; much simpler in nature than the average requirements workshop or problem-solving session. We had video links to the offshore team members, but it just wasn't good enough. The workshops with the distributed teams took twice as long as the sessions with the co-located teams and the lessons learned were nowhere near as rich.

---

[34] Mario Moussa, Madeline Boyer, and Derek Newberry, *Committed Teams: Three Steps to Inspiring Passion and Performance,* (New Jersey: Wiley, 2016), Kindle Edition, location 4297.

One of the reasons co-location is so powerful for teams is the effect of what Alistair Cockburn calls osmotic communication. *"While writing, reading, typing, or talking, we pick up traces of the ongoing sounds around, using some background listening model even though we are not consciously paying attention."* [35] This is what enables you to pick up on a conversation taking place in your surrounds that you have something to contribute to. In distributed teams the number of lost opportunities for communication are innumerable.

Another benefit of co-location is that it enables one of the most effective forms of human communication: two people, face to face, in front of a whiteboard. In his book *Agile Analytics*, Ken Collier explains this phenomenon: *"If I can see your facial expressions, hear your voice inflections, observe your gestures, and view what you are drawing on the whiteboard, I will much more accurately understand what you are trying to tell me, Furthermore, I can save a great deal of time if I can just talk directly to you about what I'm thinking rather than writing it in an e-mail or trying to explain it over the phone."* [36]

Distributed Teams

> *.. sponsors should think twice before sponsoring a*
> *geographically distributed project*
> —Alistair Cockburn, *Agile Software Development*.

I suspect at least some of you are thinking, well, that's all well and good if you can co-locate, but what about the rest of us? It is a great question for which I have no magic answers. I know, I know, I'm not helping. It is not your choice to be distributed. It is an organisational mandate. So I'm only going to ask one thing of you: before you accept distribution as a fixed constraint, challenge your assumptions.

---

[35] Cockburn, *Agile Software Development*, location 3174.

[36] Ken Collier, *Agile Analytics: A Value-Driven Approach to Business Intelligence and Data Warehousing*, (Boston: Pearson, 2012), Kindle Edition, location 1970.

Recently I heard Dr Amantha Imber give a keynote on innovation. One of her key messages was that "assumptions fence in our thinking" and that "crushing" our assumptions "breaks down the fence". She gave the example of Steve Jobs, "crushing the assumption" that a mobile phone had to have 12 buttons (think of the wildly popular Nokia handsets that predated the smart-phone).

I will also share a story of one instance in which the co-location battle was fought and won. In this particular scenario, the corporation had an 80/20 offshore/onshore policy. The design work was done onshore and the build and test work was done offshore. The model was not working. One of the IT program managers sought an exemption to bring one project team onshore to see if the quality of the work being delivered would improve. He was granted the exemption and he proved his point. Of course, this didn't result in a change in corporate policy. It didn't even result in a change to that department's approach to distribution; well, at least at first.

One distributed project after another found itself in trouble and the program manager would respond every time with an exemption request to co-locate the team onshore. And every time the delivery improved. Eventually, the entire program team had been onshored, effectively "by stealth". Strangely this also seemed to fly under the radar of the corporate governance process, as once an exemption had been granted, it would appear that there was no process by which these decisions were reviewed. So the team just stayed onshore. While this didn't ever result in a change to the corporate position, it did have a huge impact on that particular tribe.

The difference in quality was even observed by their business stakeholders who started to insist that their projects be delivered by the onshore teams, even when the cost was perceived as higher. Over time this group managed to prove that the co-located onshore delivery model was equally as cost effective as offshoring. So much so that the next time the organisation decided to look at its cost base, instead of offshoring again, the majority of this particular tribe were converted from contractors to permanent staff.

Compensation Strategies for Distributed Teams

Assuming for a moment that your constraints are fixed, and that staging a revolution is considered a career-limiting move, your next course of action should be to minimise the impact of the constraints. The best place to start is by acknowledging that a distributed team is a compromise and that when you compromise you need to compensate.

If you can, at least try and bring the team together at one physical location for a team kick-off event early in the team's life. This will aid with relationship-building and set the stage for trust among team members. Periodic co-location will also help strengthen the relationship between team members in distributed teams. This can be in the form of short regular visits for teams that are distributed in the same city, or short quarterly visits for internationally distributed teams. I have also seen onshore rotations used to help build relationships with internationally distributed teams. This can be particularly effective when the teams are physically co-located for the first three to six months.

Regardless of your approach, technology is a key enabler for distributed teams: high-quality fit for purpose technology. Think telepresence, smart boards, and some sort of team messaging client like Slack. Agile manifesto signatory, Jim Highsmith calls this "virtual colocation".[37] When thinking about virtual co-location, consider how you can create an even playing field for everyone on the team. For example, rather than some people in a meeting room and others on the phone, consider having everyone participate via the phone.

---

[37] Ken Collier, *Agile Analytics*, location 1980.

In *Team of Teams*, General Stanley McChrystal tells the story of the Joint Special Operations Task Force in the fight against Al Qaeda after 9/11. As the head of a task force distributed across more than 70 locations General McChrystal certainly faced his share of challenges dealing with distributed teams. Rather than accepting this as a constraint, he insisted on a seamless video conference every day, in which at its peak 7,000 people participated. I don't know about you, but personally I find that to be an amazing technological feat! The general couldn't have everyone co-located in Iraq but he could enable "free-flowing conversation across the force".[38]

---

[38] General Stanley McChrystal et al., *Team of Teams: New Rules of Engagement for a Complex World*, (New York: Penguin, 2015), Kindle Edition, location 4123.

Chapter Summary

In this chapter we explored how to build great teams in order to create a solid foundation for a great tribe.

- Keeping team sizes small enhances the teams' ability to communicate effectively.
- While it is okay for managers to design the teams, self-selection is a powerful approach for shaping teams that can also help to kick-start cultural change.
- Teams need clarity with respect to their authority over their work practices. A useful tool for collaboratively creating this clarity is Jurgen Appelo's Delegation Poker.
- Teams that adopt the Minimal Viable Agility practices of retrospective on cadence, visualising their work and daily communication, are more effective.
- Social contracts created early in a team's life help establish acceptable behavioural norms.
- Where possible, it is preferable for teams to be co-located, so that they can benefit from richer communication due to factors like osmotic communication and the ability to have face-to-face conversations in front of a whiteboard.
- Distributed teams are a compromise that may well be unavoidable and therefore need to be actively compensated.

Teams are critical to effective tribes. In a tribe of 100 people there are 4,950 different communication channels. Teams provide the structure that prevents chaos!

In the next section we will explore how we create a connection between teams to create Tribal Unity.

PART 2

CONNECTING TEAMS AND CREATING YOUR TRIBE

If tribes are the most powerful vehicles within companies, cultures are their engines—David Logan, *Tribal Leadership*.

There has been much written about how to create a great team culture. The concepts covered in the previous section just scrape the surface of this body of work, but it should be enough to get you started. What is less available is literature on creating a great culture across a team of teams, or perhaps as I like to term it, scaling culture and creating Tribal Unity.

We know from Seth Godin that *"A tribe is a group of people connected to one another, connected to a leader, and connected to an idea."* When we create teams we start to connect people to one another. We also need to create connections between the people across the different teams.

Shared Identity

It is very hard to have a sense of belonging to a community
when the community doesn't have a clear name and image
—Jurgen Appelo, *#Workout*.

The teams in the tribe need a shared identity; this is the first step in creating a One Team Culture. I like to start by giving the tribe a name or a theme (or both if you like!). The teams then also choose identities that align to the chosen tribal theme. Sometimes the leader chooses the theme, other times the teams nominate themes and have a vote to decide what the tribe's theme should be.

It may surprise you that I would advocate the theme being chosen by the leader. You may be thinking to yourself: "Isn't that a little dictatorial?" It may seem that way but for the leaders I work with, this can often be one of the rare times I let them make a decision that will affect their tribe! Well, at least that is how it has been explained to me!

By way of example, my first tribe was the EDW Agile Release Train (not really an amazing name, I know) but given we were a train, all the teams had train-themed names such as: Astrotrain, Thomas, Hyperloop, Jacobite, Maglev, and Soul Train. I also worked with a tribe called "StAART" (the Student Administration Agile Release Train). This tribe had a superhero team theme. The teams had names like the Avengers, the Justice League, and the Teenage Mutant Ninja Turtles. A recent favourite is a tribe that works on an application called Compass. They call their tribe the Explorers and the teams are named after famous explorers, including Neil Armstrong and Captain Cook! I could go on all day but I'm guessing you've got the point.

Names help create a sense of belonging, the same way that sporting club names, colours, and logos create a sense of community. Belonging is a fundamental human need. When we feel we belong it helps prevent our "fight or flight" reflex from kicking in.[39] The tribe's workplace should reflect its theme. The tribe's name should be big and visible. The team's names and logos should adorn the teams' workspaces. Some teams and tribes even have a mascot. StAART had a train, whereas the EDW Release Train's mascot was a skeleton called "Meh", which even participated in tribe photos. Which reminds me, always make time to take photos of your tribe!

 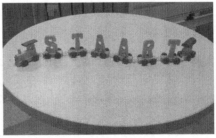

---

[39] Christine Comaford, *Smart Tribes: How Teams Become Brilliant Together,* (London: Penguin, 2013), Kindle Edition, location 239.

One of my favourite tribal identifiers is the tribe T-shirt. I desperately wanted T-shirts for my EDW tribe but I didn't think the organisation would be willing to pay for them. So one summer when I was in Bali on holidays (yes, again!), I did what all good Aussies do and brought back T-shirts for my tribe. I had them custom printed with the EDW Agile Release Train logo on the front and "World Leaders in Agile Data Warehousing" on the back.

Team as a Product Box

When establishing a new team, it is generally only a matter of time before someone decides that a team-building activity is in order. Maybe one of those trust games where someone falls and the rest of the team have to catch them. It makes me squirm in my seat just to think about it.

Back in the EDW days, Mark came up with the idea of having the teams create product boxes. This is an adaption of the product box exercise from *Innovation Games*.[40] In our variation, each team is asked to think of itself as a product and physically create the box that the team would be packaged in if it were to be sold on a supermarket shelf. The packaging should address the following questions:

---

[40] Luke Hohmann, *Innovation Games: Creating Breakthrough Products Through Collaborative Play*, (Boston: Pearson, 2007), Kindle Edition, location 1653.

- Who are your customers? (both internal and external)
- What are the key services you offer those customers?
- What are your customers saying about you?
- What are your requirements? (i.e. conditions for success)
- What sets your team apart from your competitors? (both internally and externally)

These days I include this exercise as a part of establishing the tribe. If I am running a self-selection event, I will do this activity in the afternoon of the self-selection day. All you need is the teams, some boxes, and some art-and-craft supplies. Give them the brief, set the time box, and you are good to go! When everyone is done and dusted it is time for the real fun, getting the teams to "showcase" their product box to the other teams in the tribe.

Shared Experiences

> *... vulnerability-based trust cannot be achieved overnight.*
> *It requires shared experiences over time...*
> —Patrick Lencioni,
> *The Five Dysfunctions of a Team.*

When it comes to connecting people, shared experiences are key. The team as a product box exercise is a perfect example of this. The trick is to create a ritual that enables shared experiences on a regular basis and also provides an opportunity for tribe members to interact with people in other teams in the tribe. A ritual I am fond of using for these purposes is called Unity Hour. Created by the leadership of the EDW tribe, this practice has been successfully replicated by tribes of all different types all over the world. It is this ritual that I credit with both beginning and sustaining the EDW tribe's cultural transformation.

Originally called Unity Day, the idea was the result of a failed attempt to hold a SAFe style PI Planning event.[41] While reflecting on the demise of the event the leadership team felt strongly that the biggest missed opportunity was team Unity. Sadly, despite most of the 100 people in EDW tribe having worked together on various aspects of EDW over the past couple of years, we didn't all know each other's names! The PI Planning day was going to be the first time we would bring the whole team together and it was something we had been excited about. And so Unity Hour was born! An all-hands gathering, first thing in the morning on the first day of every two-week sprint.

When I look back and think about how I would have reacted as a business sponsor if my IT counterpart had told me that he wanted the EDW delivery team to down tools for an hour once every couple of weeks, I fear I would not have been open to the idea. I would have been wrong. Having seen Unity Hour in action with technology and business teams, both Agile and not Agile, I can't think of anything

---

[41] In SAFe a PI (Program Increment) is a fixed duration development time box in the range of 8-12 weeks. Each PI commences with a two-day "all hands" PI Planning event, with full participation from both the Agile Release Train and its business stakeholders. During this session a high-level delivery plan is produced for the PI. In the case of the EDW, we did not have a funded backlog large enough to support a PI Planning event. At the time there was minimal demand for development on the EDW and we were barely keeping the full train occupied from one week to the next.

more important to the tribe's wellbeing than this one-hour escape from reality on some sort of regular cadence.

I still remember the day I realised the difference Unity Hour had made to the culture of the EDW tribe. I was walking the floor and noticed that people were in the "wrong" team areas—then I realised that it wasn't people in the wrong space, it was people collaborating across the tribe, sharing knowledge and supporting each other. I couldn't wipe the grin off my face for days.

Unity Hour Activities

Unity Hour has no fixed agenda and should evolve with new segments and activities being dreamed up all the time. The following list should help you get started building the agenda for your first Unity Hour:

Shout Outs: This is the only agenda item that has appeared at every Unity Hour I have been involved with. Ideally, this time is used to publicly appreciate people who have supported you or your team during the previous time box, which is generally followed by a huge round of applause. It is an amazing and uplifting experience to observe. Shout outs can be given by anyone to anybody regardless of whether they are a member of the tribe.

Some tribes have supported the "shout outs" with a Kudo Box.[42] Between Unity Hours, team members would write their shout out on a Kudo Card and put it in the Kudo Box. Then each Unity Hour, the box would be emptied, the kudos read out to the tribe and then posted on a wall for people to read later.

---

[42] Jurgen Appelo, *Managing for Happiness: Games, Tools, and Practices to Motivate Any Team*, (New Jersey: Wiley, 2016), Kindle Edition, chapter 1.

Learning Activities/Games: With Unity Hour being an all-hands meeting, it provides a fantastic opportunity for shared learning. Of course, finding games or activities that scale is always a challenge. The Tasty Cupcakes website[43] is an excellent resource when looking for learning games. My friend Mark also highly recommends the Agile Games conference[44] as a source of inspiration.

Here is a list of activities I have seen used successfully at a Unity Hour:

- **Ball point game:** Commonly used in Scrum training this game requires the tribe to split into teams and pass balls around the team while adhering to some simple rules. Playing with tennis balls can add some additional fun as they bounce away when they are dropped, adding to the chaos. [45]
- **The penny game**: Often used to teach Lean concepts, this game involves forming teams that flip pennies in different-sized batches, then comparing the results. Like with the ball game, expect a little bit of chaos as coins get accidentally flipped off tables or even into coffee cups. [46]
- **Invisible maze**: This one takes a bit of set-up as you need to create a physical grid on the floor for each team. We usually use painter's tape for this. Each team is given a manager, who has a map of the maze and can only provide feedback in the form of a "beep" when a team member steps out of the maze. This exercise is sure to get everyone thinking! [47]
- **Agile airplane game**: In this game the teams get to be a paper-airplane-building factory. The fun really begins when it comes time for the test flights. Only planes that can fly for at least two

---

[43] See: http://tastycupcakes.org/

[44] See: http://www.agilegamesnewengland.com/

[45] See: http://dpwhelan.com/blog/uncategorized/learning-scrum-through-the-ball-point-game/

[46] See: http://tastycupcakes.org/2013/05/the-penny-game/

[47] See: http://www.youtube.com/watch?v=VeoQ9weTWPw

metres are accepted and rejected planes are torn up and thrown away. This one is worth playing just for the fun of seeing grown adults get very serious about the quality of paper airplanes. [48]

- **Chair game:** In this game you split the tribe into three groups giving each group different instructions that at first seem to be contradictory but with a little bit of cooperation can all be solved with a single solution. A word of warning on this one: some people may get very passionate about the placement of the chairs resulting in a tug of war, so I suggest you have some referees on standby to keep things civilised. [49]

- **Musical chairs:** This group puzzle works for groups of 25-30 people, so you will probably need to split your tribe up to play this game. It involves the group keeping the facilitator from sitting in an empty chair. It always seems easy in theory but will often take groups up to an hour to solve. [50]

- **The marshmallow challenge:** This is another puzzle that seems simple at face value. Teams of four are given 18 minutes to build the tallest possible free-standing structure they can using just: "20 sticks of spaghetti, one yard of tape, one yard of string, and one marshmallow. The marshmallow needs to be on top." [51]

To increase the tribe's integration, randomly generate groups for each activity. One simple approach is handing out a deck of playing cards as people arrive then getting them to form groups based on the number or suit of their card. Another trick is having people line up in an order, perhaps the month of their birthday or the date, then have them count off into groups.

---

[48] See: http://gistlabs.com/2011/06/agile-airplane-game/

[49] See: http://agiletrail.com/2012/03/27/8-great-short-games-for-groups/

[50] See: http://www.agilenotanarchy.com/2016/07/agile-musical-chairs-facilitation-guide.html

[51] See: http://www.tomwujec.com/design-projects/marshmallow-challenge/

Team Building Activities: You can also include activities that are less focused on learning and more about team building and fun. The team product box exercise is one example of this. Team Hakas are also a lot of fun. I have also seen a tribe perform the Macarena in an attempt to win a corporate contest! When it comes to competition the Corporate Games[52] can be a fun day out.

---

[52] See: http://www.corporategames.net.au/

The Power of Haka

According to Wikipedia, the Haka "is a traditional war cry, dance or challenge ... performed by a group, with vigorous movements and stamping of the feet with rhythmically shouted accompaniment."[53] When I attended Dean Leffingwell's SAFe Program Consultant (SPC) course he used a video of the New Zealand All Blacks[54] performing a haka to illustrate "The Power of Ba", "ba" being the place teams are in when they are high performing, self-organising and energised. If you have not seen an All Blacks haka before there are a number of examples readily available on YouTube. Have a look for yourself and I'm sure you will agree that the spine-chilling performances are the perfect illustration of what it feels like to be part of a team that has truly reached "ba", a place where "we, the work and the knowledge are one".

During the SPC class Dean also shared videos he had received from his clients where their teams had created their own team hakas. I loved it, and it led me to contemplate how I might convince my teams to invent and perform their own haka.

I started my campaign for a "Haka Challenge" by talking to my leadership team, who responded with mixed emotions: "Excellent idea!", "You can't make me do the haka on my birthday!", and "Do we have to?". Not deterred by the detractors I took the idea to the scrum masters who didn't exactly bounce off the walls with excitement, but were willing to give it a try and thought it could be fun. With the scrum masters on board I pitched the idea for a "Haka Challenge" to the

---

[53] Wikipedia, *Haka*, accessed 10th October 2016, https://en.wikipedia.org/wiki/Haka.

[54] The All Blacks are New Zealand's national rugby union team. They are considered the most successful team ever to play the game. See: https://en.wikipedia.org/wiki/New_Zealand_national_rugby_union_team

entire EDW tribe, giving all the teams a Sprint to prepare a haka for a "Hak-off" at our next Unity Hour.

Some teams were immediately inspired while others were very reluctant, but over the course of the fortnight they all got in to it. The laughter from haka planning sessions could be heard through meeting room walls and there was a quiet buzz on the floor as teams went about practising hakas while also trying to keep the content a secret.

When the day of the Haka Challenge arrived there was an air of anticipation as the teams gathered for Unity Hour. There was face paint, skirts made of Post-it-note-covered butchers paper, and a large contingent proudly sporting their "EDW Release Train" T-shirts. Each team had its own unique flavour. One wrote their haka in Maori, another learnt an actual authentic haka; there was even a team that created a haka inspired by the EDW architecture![55]

The flow-on effect from the "Hak-off" was like magic. I had started out wanting to enhance team "ba" and ended up creating "ba" across the entire train, as highlighted to me in an e-mail I received from one of my scrum masters the next morning:

> *Since doing the haka exercise—and aside from the fact that I lost my voice...*
>
> *Everyone across teams has been congratulatory of the other teams and their members. It has instilled a massive cross pollination of communication and engagement going on!!!*

---

[55] Videos of some of the EDW hakas can be viewed at: http://www.pretty-agile.com/2013/05/the-power-of-haka.html

The quieter team members from various teams across the department are having animated corridor conversations.

The level of talking and noise being generated in the different team areas has been much, much higher, even late into the night!

Further, people are far less tense and defensive in the general discussions across the department. People are open and honest, after having embarrassed themselves.

Basically, the teams are showing greater interest, engagement, and "hunger" for what they do, and what they are about...

How do you quantify all of this? You don't, but what I do know is that the teams are more galvanised, and have a much stronger sense of their own context ... and being part of the greater whole: being EDW!!!

Four years on this Unity Hour is still the highlight of my time with the EDW tribe.

Note: While this event was well intended, when I shared this story at a conference in 2013, I was informed via Twitter that it is culturally offensive to New Zealanders to do a haka as a "fun Agile team building thing". In my defence, I did not know and in my view what we did was intended as an homage. Since then I have completed some additional research[56] and I am comfortable that what we did was in the right spirit so I have included it here an illustration of what is possible when it comes to creating Tribal Unity.

---

[56] See: https://en.wikipedia.org/wiki/Cultural_appropriation

Fundraising: A wonderful side effect of Unity Hour is the opportunity that it provided tribe members to raise awareness and increase participation in the charitable fundraising activities they are involved with. My favourite has to be Movember.[57] While the moustaches are often amusing, with the EDW tribe, it was the "parade of the mos" ceremony culminating in the dot voting (by sticking dots on the guys) for the best mo that made this event stand out for me. One year one of the guys

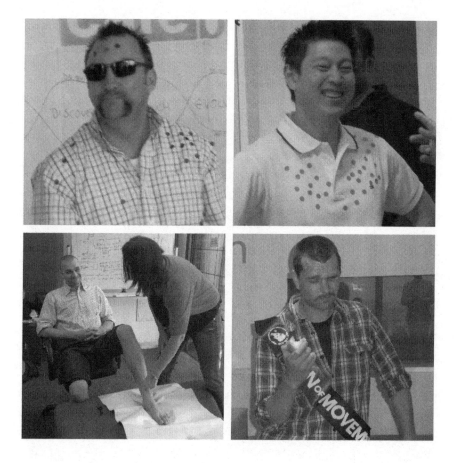

---

[57] For those not familiar with this, it is men (and women) raising money for prostate cancer and men's suicide prevention by growing moustaches during November.

committed to eating a raw onion at Unity Hour if we helped him reach his fundraising target, which of course we did! Another highlight was the time that our raw-onion-eating fundraiser told the tribe that if we raised $1500 for Shave for a Cure we could wax his legs in the office. So we did!

Team Updates: Sometimes the tribe just wants to know more about what is going on across all the teams in the tribe. I have seen Unity Hour used for this purpose, but you need to be careful you don't turn Unity Hour into a boring fortnightly status meeting. To liven things up, I have witnessed teams use short skits, slideshows put to music, and even Pictionary to share their team highlights from the last period. Just remember to time box! One particularly memorable Unity Hour was when one of the Scrum masters orchestrated an Agile X-Factor, where team updates were rated on according to their "A-Factor".

Theme Days: Now and then just for fun embrace a theme, whether it be "International Talk Like a Pirate Day", Halloween, or Christmas: it always keeps things interesting.

Snacks: Regardless of the agenda for the day, if you want to keep 100-odd people focused at 9:00 a.m. in the morning, provide food! Linda Rising calls this pattern "do food". She states in her book *Fearless Change*: *"Research shows that we become fonder for people and things we experience while we are eating."*[58] I realise you may not have access to a "food budget" but don't let this deter you. Find the bakers in your tribes and enlist their help. If you are lucky they may even be willing to support your fundraising efforts with "ginger mo men". Or stop by the donut store on the way to the office and shout the tribe a few boxes of donuts.

One of the reasons Unity Hour is so powerful is that it creates a safe environment for tribe members to display their vulnerability. This is key as vulnerability is the foundation of trust and trust is the foundation of great teams.

Breakaway Day

Another ritual invented by the rather creative EDW tribe was called Breakaway Day. This was an annual event, held on the last day of work before the end-of-year break.[59] Breakaway Day was always held in one of Melbourne's beautiful public gardens. The day started with the "track and field events": sack races, egg-and-spoon races, three-legged races, and wheelbarrow races all being included in the mix. After the games there would be pizza and beer, with many tribe members hanging out together at the park until early evening. It is important to note that this was a proper paid work day, not some sort of compulsory unpaid love-in!

---

[58] Mary Lynn Manns and Linda Rising, *Fearless Change: Patterns for Introducing New Ideas*, (Boston: Pearson, 2005), Kindle Edition, location 2539.

[59] In Australia it is common for businesses to shut down at the end of the year from late December, just before Christmas until early January, after New Year's Day.

Cocktail Hour

When people share rhythms with others they develop stronger
emotional bonds and are more likely to pitch in for the common good
— Robert I. Sutton and Huggy Rao, *Scaling Up Excellence*.

Of course there is more to connecting the tribe than getting together to play games every couple of weeks. We need rituals that connect the tribe every day. My good friend Wayne Palmer came up with the idea of Cocktail Hour after reading about the "Daily Cocktail Party" in Henrik Kniberg's *Lean From the Trenches*. In essence, Cocktail Hour is a series of cascading daily stand-ups that culminate in a daily cross-tribe stand-up. The specific format will vary from tribe to tribe; however, I recommend trying to keep it to an hour and ideally holding it first thing in the morning.

I have to admit I thought Wayne was losing the plot when he cooked up Cocktail Hour, but he wasn't, it was pure gold. Prior to its existence, I used to torture everyone, including myself, with a weekly three-hour progress meeting every Monday morning. Twenty-five people and a 100-page status report made for a very long start to the week!

The EDW tribe used the following agenda; it should be enough to at least get you started:
9:00 a.m. Leadership Stand-up
9:15 a.m. Delivery Team Stand-ups
9:30 a.m. Tribe Sync[60]
9:45 a.m. Support Team Stand-ups

---

[60] For the agilists out there this is similar to a Scrum of Scrums or a SAFe ART sync.

The leadership stand-up was an informal daily touch base that enabled the tribe's leadership to align on priorities for the day ahead. The two types of team stand-ups were a reflection of the two types of teams in the tribe: the delivery teams that worked on our core mission and the support teams that provide services to the teams. We wanted the delivery teams to talk first so that they could bring any issues or blockers to the Tribe Sync. The support teams could then take the relevant problems into their stand-ups and factor them into their priorities for the day ahead.

This ritual ran every day except on Unity Day. For me the Tribe Sync is the heartbeat of the tribe. Every morning people from across the tribe share their progress and challenges with their peers. Visitors at EDW were always quick to comment on both how transparent everyone was and on the energy of the team. This stand-up was always peppered with lots of good-humoured jibes and comedic antics designed to start the day with a laugh. Of course the real magic is the speed of the information flow. Within the first hour of the day, all the blockers across all the teams have been surfaced and the remedial actions have commenced.

Create a Whole of Tribe View

When you visualize your pain and gather data about it, it's much
easier to get the stakeholders' and other teams' understanding.
It's not you nagging, it's data
—Marcus Hammarberg and Joakim Sundén,
Kanban in Action.

The secret to an effective Tribe Sync is having an effective visualisation to support it. Whatever you do, don't over-engineer this. You want to be able to see at the macro level what work each team has in progress. It can also be useful to see what they have queued up to do next and what they have completed. The discussion at the Tribe Sync should be focused on where teams are experiencing challenges and identifying who can help them move forward. We don't need to solve the problems at the Tribe Sync, we just need to make the connections across the tribe.

How do you know if you have your visualisation right? Good visualisation leads to good conversation. If you can't have or aren't having the conversations you want in front of the wall, evolve your visualisation. Effective walls are forever being torn down and replaced as the tribe learns and grows. [61]

---

[61] See: http://www.prettyagile.com/2015/03/leaning-into-safe-with-feature-flow.html

Chapters and Guilds

*If each squad was fully autonomous and had
no communication with other squads, then what is the point of having a
company? Spotify might as well be chopped into 30 different small companies*
—Henrik Kniberg and Anders Ivarsson,
Scaling Agile @ Spotify.

The concept of chapters and guilds is not unlike the idea of communities of practice. If you have formed cross-functional teams[62] as recommended in Part 1 then it is likely that those with specialist skills have been distributed across the various teams in your tribe. This can prove challenging for organisations if something is not done to maintain a connection between people with the same specialisation so that they continue to grow their expertise in their chosen domain.

At the online streaming music company, Spotify, they solve this with chapters and guilds. This was another idea Wayne read about while we were working with the EDW tribe. After reading about chapters and guilds in the *Scaling Agile @ Spotify* paper by Henrik Kniberg and Anders Ivarsson, he proposed we form a series of "guilds" across the tribe. Wayne was keen to see the tribe take ownership of the quality of what it delivered and more specifically to "put the control and responsibility for core specialisations into the hands of the people who are doing the work, in order to restore a sense of pride and satisfaction within their work". This mission was premised on the deeply held belief that "to achieve true continuous improvement, the value stream needs to be owned, understood, and improved upon by the people closest to it".

It was our hope that people with expertise in specific skill sets would meet regularly, in order to:

---

[62] Teams that contain all the skills needed for the squad to deliver on its mission.

- share knowledge
- create tools
- create training material and conduct training
- set standards and practices
- review changes in tools, techniques, and methods
- take an outside-in view of the system (the way the work works)

It had always puzzled me why Wayne chose to start a discussion about guilds rather than chapters. For those who have not read the *Scaling Agile @ Spotify* paper the definitions are as follows:

- A chapter "is your small family of people having similar skills and working within the same general competency area, within the same tribe."
- "A guild is a more organic and wide-reaching 'community of interest', a group of people that want to share knowledge, tools, code, and practices."
- Where a tribe is "a collection of squads that work in related areas" and a squad is "similar to a Scrum team".
- Noting that: "chapters are always local to a tribe, while a guild usually cuts across the whole organisation."[63]

Therefore, I figured when you have a single tribe you need chapters but not guilds. Later Wayne explained to me that he had wanted guilds as he wanted to be inclusive of everyone, not just the specialists for the given specialisation.

When implementing chapters in the tribes I work with there have been two main approaches. The first is more closely aligned to the approach used at Spotify where the chapter leads are also the line managers for the people in the chapters. I have found this to be particularly useful when working with tribes that have historically been structured by functional specialisation with a line manager for each

---

[63] Kniberg and Ivarsson, *Scaling Agile @ Spotify*

function. The alternative approach is to simply nominate chapter leads. This could be done by the tribe's leadership or by the chapters themselves (which would be my preference!).

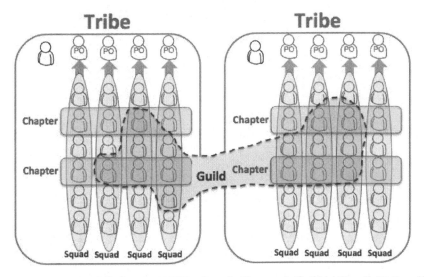

Source: *Scaling Agile @ Spotify with Tribes, Squads, Chapters & Guilds* by Henrik Kniberg[64]

Regardless of the approach, you should be clear in your expectation of the chapters. My rule of thumb is to suggest that the chapters gather together twice a week with two distinct purposes. The aim of the first session is peer review. Chapter members should bring along the work they are doing to share with their peers the approach they are taking and seek feedback. The second session tends to be less structured, perhaps a Lean Coffee style meeting, where hot topics are discussed.[65]

---

[64] See: http://blog.crisp.se/2012/11/14/henrikkniberg/scaling-agile-at-spotify

[65] "Lean Coffee is a structured, but agenda-less meeting. Participants gather, build an agenda, and begin talking. Conversations are directed and productive because the agenda for the meeting was democratically generated." See: *http://leancoffee.org/*

Many of the tribes I work with integrate their chapters into Unity Hour and Cocktail Hour. At Unity Hour, chapters will often present updates on what they are working on or share messages about new tools, techniques, or standards with the broader tribe. Depending on the nature of the chapter's work, it may also make sense to have a daily sync as part of Cocktail Hour. This would normally be scheduled after the team stand-up and before the Tribe Sync.

Celebrate as a Tribe

*When you've celebrated moving from 1 to 2, and then from 2 to 3,
you gain confidence that you can make the next advance*
—Chip and Dan Heath, Switch.

Celebrating is another great way to create connections between teams. When doing so it is important to remember to celebrate as a tribe, not individual teams. The notion that the tribe succeeds and fails as one, not as individual teams, needs to become part of the tribe's DNA. Celebrations don't always have to be related to day-to-day business. You can and should celebrate birthdays, milestones, holidays, or even International Talk Like a Pirate Day if you so wish. Just think about this for a minute: if you have a tribe of 100 people you can probably manage to have birthday cake roughly twice a week every week of the year! And we already know that when we "do food" we become fonder of one another. It's win-win!

When considering milestones there are the more traditional end-of-project celebrations, or when I worked in finance the end of financial year always seemed to be a cause for celebration. However, not every milestone needs to be delivery or outcome focused. With the EDW tribe we celebrated our first 50 Sprints with a day of festivities including a table soccer tournament and many, many rounds of Wii Rock Band.

Don't forget to celebrate the small wins every day, week, and month. Be vigilant, recognise every little forward step your tribe marks. "When you spot movement you have got to reinforce it".[66] We have already talked about shout outs and the Kudo Box. One tribe I work with has stepped this up another notch and includes shout outs in their daily Tribe Sync! Celebrating the small wins creates hope that things are changing for the better.[67]

Tribal Kaizen

Kaizen is about changing the way things are.
If you assume that things are all right the way they are,
you can't do kaizen. So change something!
—Taiichi Ohno.

Kaizen is a Japanese word that literally translated means "change for better". The spirit of kaizen as used in Lean is "continuous improvement". If you have implemented the Minimal Viable Agility practices suggested in Part 1, then your tribe's teams are already halfway there. To build a great tribe we need to add one more ingredient: a ritual I call the Bubble Up, the idea being that we ask the teams to "bubble up"

---

[66] Chip Heath and Dan Heath, *Switch: How to Change Things When Change is Hard*, (London: Random House, 2010), Kindle Edition, location 3634.

[67] Chip Heath and Dan Heath, *Switch*, location 2167.

the challenges identified in their retrospectives that are outside their sphere of influence.[68]

Like the regular team retrospectives this ritual should happen on cadence. I prefer every two weeks but every three or four weeks would work too. This works best when it is synchronised with the retrospective cadence of the teams. The session should take no longer than half an hour. Each team sends a delegate with the issues the team has identified as outside their sphere of influence. The chapter leads and the tribe's leadership team should also attend.

When we introduced this practice at EDW, we started by having the tribe bringing their challenges to the leadership team for them to resolve. It was not long before we were drowning in issues. This is when we decided to include the chapter leads; after all, every good leader knows that you can't do everything yourself! The issues were visualised on a wall (of course) and the leaders of the tribe and the

[68] Some teams like to use the "Circles and Soup" retrospective format to aid with collecting this data: http://www.futureworksconsulting.com/blog/2010/07/26/circles-and-soup/

chapters would take ownership of resolving the issues. Then one day a little bit of magic happened: as each team shared its challenges, members of the other teams pitched in with solutions they had used to solve similar problems.

When I started using this practice it was more about connecting the tribe to a leader (which is the topic of our next chapter). While this is still true, over time I have found that the true power of the ritual is in how a self-organising team of teams, supporting each other, reinforces the tribe's One Team Culture.

Accelerating Tribal Unity With a SAFe Quick-Start

The Scaled Agile Framework, also known as SAFe, is an approach to taking Agile beyond a single team, to a team of Agile teams, or even teams of teams of Agile teams. It is used primarily by software development and Lean systems engineering groups of anything from 50 to thousands of people.

The Agile Release Train is the primary organisational construct in SAFe. It is a virtual team of Agile teams of 50-125 people with a shared mission who plan, commit, and execute on a fixed cadence of 8-12 weeks.[69] While this way of working came from the world of software development the basic construct of the Agile Release Train can be used to improve the performance of any tribe and is completely congruent with all the material contained in this book. The SAFe Quick-Start approach to launching an Agile Release Train is actually an excellent way to accelerate the creation of Tribal Unity.

---

[69] See: http://scaledagileframework.com/agile-release-train/

While there is a lot of work that goes into getting prepared for a Quick-Start, the mechanics of this one-week immersion event are:
- Two days of team level training
- A two-day all-hands planning workshop
- One day of role specific training[70]

At this point, I realise that you are thinking I have completely lost the plot. This sounds like utter madness, I know. I thought it was madness too, until I tried it and realised it was truly amazing. [71]

So what does all of this have to do with Tribal Unity? At the beginning of the week, you most likely have somewhere between five and twelve newly formed teams. All the teams attend the two-day training at the same time in their teams. Everyone hears exactly the same message from the same trainers. Over the course of these first two days the teams start to bond in their individual teams as well as a team of teams, or a tribe.

Then the teams roll straight into two days of planning—together! Working in their team and as a team of teams, they continue to bond. At the end of these two very intense days, the team of teams has co-created a plan for their work over the next few months that has been accepted by their stakeholders. When it comes to shared experiences, these four days are a perfect enabler for Tribal Unity.

Recently, I have even gone so far as to run this as a six-day event, with the first day being a team self-selection workshop. Even if you are not doing software development or Lean systems engineering, perhaps you should consider "quick-starting" your way to Tribal Unity.

---

[70] For Scrum masters and product owners

[71] If you would like to learn more, you can read the case study from a quick-start I facilitated last year: http://scaledagileframework.com/westpac-case-study/

Chapter Summary

In this chapter we explored techniques for connecting teams and creating tribes.

- A shared identity for the teams and the tribe forges a connection across teams.
- Shared experiences, like Unity Hour, creates connections between team members in different teams, strengthening the connection of the tribe.
- A daily Cocktail Hour is one way to provide daily connection and alignment across the tribe.
- Visualising the tribes work helps with creating shared understanding of interdependences between teams.
- Chapters and guilds help maintain connection between specialists in a tribe of cross-functional teams.
- Tribes succeed and fail as one. This should be reflected in how you celebrate.
- For your tribe to continue to get better and better you need to implement tribal kaizen rituals like the Bubble Up.
- The SAFe Quick-Start provides a template for accelerating connection within and across teams.

It is this connection between teams that fuels the creation of a One Team Culture.

In the next section we will explore how we create a connection between the tribe and its leader.

PART 3

CONNECTING TO A LEADER

Tribes need leadership—Seth Godin, *Tribes.*

Now that you know how to create connections within the tribe, let's look at how we create a connection between the tribe and its leader. Creating Tribal Unity begins and ends with leadership; however, connecting leaders to tribes is not as simple as you may think. It is as if there is an invisible wall between the people who do the work and their leaders and it works both ways. The leaders think they are intruding if they visit a team space or sit in on a workshop. The teams think the leader isn't spending time with the team because the leader just doesn't care. In most cases leaders really do care about their teams and what is happening with them but it is hard to care about things you aren't aware of.

Be Part of the Change

> *It is not enough that management commit themselves to quality and productivity, they must know what it is they must do. Such a responsibility cannot be delegated*
> —W. Edwards Deming.

If you are a leader and you are reading this book, you may be considering making changes to your organisation with a view to creating Tribal Unity and a One Team Culture. If you think that you can go and hire yourself a consultant and perhaps pay for some training for your team and Tribal Unity will emerge—sorry, that's just not how this works. This is what my friend Jean Tabaka called a "chequebook commitment".

Don't get me wrong, I have been a general manager in a large enterprise, I know how hard it can be to get funding for consulting and training, but I also know it is just not enough. I have worked with teams whose leaders have written a cheque and then checked out and it is just awful. The teams were forever asking me where their leader was and why they were not participating in the training or workshop that was in progress. The bottom line is, if you want to achieve Tribal Unity, you are going to have to get off the sidelines and head into the fray!

Leaders who excel at creating Tribal Unity are there every step of the way. They show their teams how serious they are about making a change by getting involved, being present, even sitting through team level training. I know you are busy, I know this isn't easy, but if you invest the time now, you will be paid back in spades once your tribe is established and humming. In the end, it's your call. Your tribe will read from your behaviour your level of commitment to this change. What do you want them to see?

Train Everyone!

No goal, regardless of how small,
can be achieved without adequate training
—Taiichi Ohno.

Speaking of training, if you are going to change the way your people work you have a moral obligation to provide them with adequate training and support to make the change. This is not negotiable. You cannot expect people to behave differently if you don't give them the skills and the context to do so. In the case of Tribal Unity, this means giving the teams the know-how to implement the Minimal Viable Agility practices covered in Part 1.

Connect at the Gemba

Farming looks mighty easy when your plow is a
pencil and you're 1,000 miles from the corn field
—Dwight Eisenhower.

Taiichi Onho, the father of the Toyota Production System, is also considered to be the creator of the gemba walk. Gemba is a Japanese word meaning "the real place". To "go to the gemba" is to "go to the real place" where the work is done. Or to put it simply, go and spend time with your tribe in its natural habitat.

If you are like me and spend most of your working life in office buildings, then you might be questioning the wisdom of walking around an office floor filled with people with their eyes glued to computer screens. It certainly doesn't sound very entertaining. This is where those physical visualisations we discussed in Part 1 come into play. If the teams have effective information radiators, walking the floor should provide you with a wealth of information about your tribe.

I was first introduced to this concept when I was the business sponsor of the EDW program. Mark was convinced that the program status meetings were a waste of time. In his view there was a deeply embedded culture of fear that was preventing the teams from telling the real story. He was adamant that if I spent more time with the teams I would be able to see this for myself.

I remember being mildly insulted by the insinuation that my relationships with the teams weren't strong enough for them to feel comfortable enough telling me about their challenges, but eventually I got over myself and went to observe some team stand-ups. For the most part these stand-ups made no sense to me. I remember going back to Mark and telling him, "It's technobabble. I have no idea what they are talking about. I am always greeted with smiles and I smile back, but I just don't understand the content."

Mark's next idea was to block out two hours in my diary to "walk the walls". This involved visiting every team in their team space. This too was pleasant enough. I could at least understand the conversation so that was a big plus. However, I still didn't feel like I was learning much about the challenges the teams were facing.

Again I gave Mark my feedback on his grand plan. He told me to try it again and this time I should ask the teams, "How can I help you?" Guess what? It worked! Many of the problems that the teams were facing were actually trivial from my perspective. I can remember talking to someone who had found it easier to hook up his personal laptop to the corporate network than it was for him to get a computer with enough grunt to do his job! As a GM all I had to do was send an email or make a phone call and a new computer was ordered.

"Walking the walls" had an added bonus for me. It helped me build rapport with the teams. They would give me problems to solve and it was my job to earn their trust by taking action. Later Mark would tell me that part of his motivation in getting me to walk the walls was to help the team see I was "human". He said, "I want them to see the Em that I see, when we are hanging out debating issues in your office."

A word of warning: whatever you do, don't go and visit your teams and ask them, "What are you doing?" This will have the complete opposite effect and likely put them on the defensive. Instead of making connections you could well alienate your tribe, if they misinterpret your genuine interest in their work as micromanagement!

Cadence based all hands planning workshops[72] are a fantastic way to manufacture gemba time. All the teams in your tribe spend two-days together in a large room with their leaders planning out the work they will be doing for the next two to three months. For many leaders this is the first time they have seen the reality of what it is like to work in the tribe. For some it may be the first time they have met the people who actually do all the work. I can remember one business sponsor

---

[72] Such as SAFe's two-day PI Planning events held on an 8, 10 or 12 week cadence.

commenting that before her first PI Planning workshop that she had "often wondered if developers were mythical beings."[73]

Understand the System of Work

To manage one must lead. To lead, one must understand the work that he and his people are responsible for
—W. Edwards Deming.

Often people who lead organisations are not actually subject matter experts. Take me, for example, the business person who ended up leading a technology team. For starters, I don't code, at all. Nor do I know how to do data modelling, test automation, or a raft of other really valuable skills that equate to getting the real work done. (I would like it noted that on several occasions I have offered to help my teams out with real work but for some strange reason they really haven't been keen on the idea …) So this poses the question: what value do I add to organisations I lead?

It is my fundamental belief that the role of management is to support the people who do the work. To do this you need to understand the system of work. Lean leaders use a tool called Value Stream Mapping to understand how the work works. I think John Shook and Mike Rother described the value of this approach perfectly when they named their book on this subject: *Learning to See.*

When it comes to understanding the flow of work in an office environment, Karen Martin's book *Value Stream Mapping* is the go-to re-

---

[73] See: http://www.prettyagile.com/2014/09/SAFe-ART-PSI-release-planning.html

source.[74] Her approach is to facilitate a workshop with the managers that "own" steps in the process she is mapping. The managers "go to the gemba" and observe how the work is being done then come back and visualise it on a wall. Usually, just the act of visualising the end-to-end process and making it accessible will improve the flow of work through a system. Without fail the participants will also discover inefficiency and duplication in the process. Imagine being part of a tribe's leadership team and being able to tell them you have reviewed all the red tape and hoops they have to jump through and have taken action to remove the non-value-adding waste. The connection you get from that announcement might even manifest itself in a hug!

Take Responsibility for the Way the Work Works

People are already doing their best; the problems are with the system.
Only management can change the system
—W. Edwards Deming.

Leaders are often surprised when they learn what is actually going on in their organisations. I know the first time I saw a value stream map for development on the EDW, I was shocked by the process. But once I could see it I could take action and that is exactly what I did. Despite not being at all technical, with the help of my tribe I was able to lobby for funding to invest in automating many of our antiquated technical processes. The key was being able to show the holders of the purse strings how automation would reduce manual effort and subsequently, the cost of delivery.

---

[74] Karen Martin and Mike Osterling, *Value Stream Mapping: How to Visualize Work and Align Leadership for Organizational Transformation*, (McGraw-Hill, 2014), Kindle Edition.

Another approach I have seen a leader use to take responsibility for the work of their tribe was in the form of a booth at a SAFe PI Planning event. The tribe's leader recognised that his tribe was overloaded with customer requests that required manual intervention on a regular basis. He told his tribe to look at this "business as usual" (BAU) work and if they thought it might be able to be stopped with his support, that they should come and see him at his booth. The booth was set up with a big visible sign offering to "Offload your BAU!" He had a number of visitors that morning but he later told me that the best part was that the tribe had continued to bring him work that they perceived as waste post the event and they were continuing to reduce this burden on the tribe.

Every Tribe Needs a Great Leadership Team

> *... the only way to systematically ensure that you have*
> *great people at every level is to ensure that you have great leaders at every level*
> *—leaders who make the people around them better*
> —James Parker, CEO, Southwest Airlines.

So far in this section we have talked a lot about the role of the leader in solving problems for the tribe, but no leader can solve all the problems of the tribe on their own. Every tribal leader needs a strong team of lieutenants. I cannot stress enough how important this is to building a great tribe. If you don't instinctively know who these people are you probably don't have them yet, so it is time to go and find them!

Once you have found your lieutenants you need to make them a team. When introducing a change to the way a tribe works it is easy for the management team to expect the tribe to change while not truly understanding what this change means on a day-to-day practical level. Leaders run the risk of confusing their understanding of the theory with a true appreciation of what it means to operate as an Agile team. So it follows that all the things that we said about teams in Part 1 holds true for leadership teams too, especially the expectation that they will embrace the Minimal Viable Agile practices. This may be more challenging than it seems at face value.

When I tried this with the EDW leadership team we had a kanban board with all the tasks that we needed to complete and held daily stand-ups, but we didn't have the discipline to make the time to action the tasks! Personally, it never ceases to amaze me how difficult it is to get Agile leaders to operate as an Agile team. It would seem many leaders are much better at instructing others on how to be Agile than they are at walking the talk!

Over time we slowly improved our processes but we never achieved the same level of effectiveness of the core delivery teams. We settled on two visualisations to support the leadership team. Firstly, an "Ops" board filled with Post-its that represented the tasks we were working on from a day-to-day, operational perspective. Supported by the daily stand-up at the beginning of Cocktail Hour this was designed to help us communicate our focus for the day ahead and debate priorities when there was misalignment. The second board was our Continuous Improvement wall that visualised the big ticket items that we were leading on behalf of the tribe. The wall contained handwritten cards with only a few words to indicate the essence of the idea and a simple "Plan, Do, Check, Spanked" kanban board (spanked being our version of done). This second board was maintained as part of our weekly Lean Coffee style team meeting.

The Role of the Leadership Team is to Serve the Tribe

*To lead is to serve. Remember that. Every single outstanding
leader that ever was, is, and shall be understands that
greatness is found in serving*
—Keni Thomas, *Get it On!*.

Now that you have whipped your team of lieutenants into shape, it is time to put them to work in service of your tribe. Hopefully, you have been at the gemba and running your Bubble Ups on cadence, so you have no shortage of problems to solve and ways to serve your tribe. It is critical that you and your lieutenants follow through here.

When working with the EDW tribe I ended up extremely frustrated about the lack of issues bubbling to the surface. I was baffled. Only the very worst teams have nothing to improve and while we weren't perfect, surely we weren't that bad! Eventually one of the teams 'fessed up. The tribe had lost faith in us. The response to my questions about why issues weren't being surfaced: "There is no point. We tell you stuff and no one follows through." Ouch!

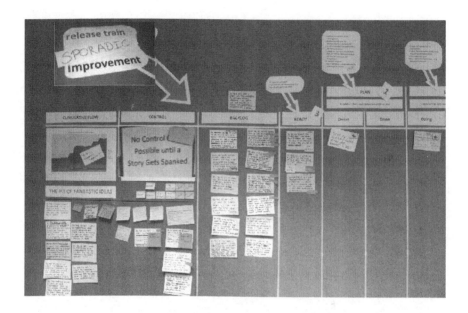

While it took us a long time to become effective, our leadership continuous improvement kanban board kept us honest. It also allowed the tribe to hold us to account and comment on our lack of delivery! It was this particular comment that resulted in the Bubble Up being reshaped to include participation by both the tribe's leadership and the chapter leads. The fortnightly Bubble Up helped keep us focused, as everyone would witness both our commitment to resolving issues and our progress or lack of progress. There is nothing quite like having leaders be transparent with the people that they serve when it comes to enhancing their sense of responsibility to the tribe.

PI Planning events also provide a wonderful opportunity for leaders to serve their tribe. This is built into the standard PI Planning agenda through the "Management Review & Problem Solving" session. [75] During day one of the planning workshop the tribe surfaces all the things that will impede their ability to deliver to the plan. At the end of the day, after the tribe members have headed home for a well-earned rest, the leadership stays back in service of the tribe. This is the "Management Review & Problem Solving" session. It is here that the leaders are tasked with removing impediments for the tribe. The next morning the leaders report back to the tribe on the actions they have taken to clear the path for the tribe. The effectiveness of this practice not only reinforces the role of the leader in serving the tribe, but also highlights the power of leaders spending time at the gemba.

Carve Out Time for Innovation

The ultimate freedom *for creative groups is the freedom to*
experiment with new ideas. Some skeptics insist that innovation is expensive.
In the long run, innovation is cheap.
Mediocrity is expensive—and autonomy can be the antidote
—Tom Kelley, General Manager, IDEO.

If you have not watched the video summary of Daniel Pink's book *Drive: The Surprising Truth About What Motivates Us,* you have to do this! [76] The basic premise is that people are intrinsically motivated, which means that they like work that gives them a sense of autonomy, mastery, and purpose. Think about Wikipedia, a company with very few employees but where thousands of people volunteer their time to grow and maintain it for free! How cool is that?!

---

[75] See: http://scaledagileframework.com/pi-planning/

[76] Link for RSA Animate video of Daniel Pink's book *Drive: The Surprising Truth About What Motivates Us* https://youtu.be/u6XAPnuFjJc

So if we accept the premise that people want to do "innovative, challenging work", we should create a work environment that enables this. The approach I have tended to use is Innovation Time. Based on Google's 20 percent time[77] the idea is that everyone can spend 10% of their working life on innovation. I always take a very liberal interpretation of innovation; for example, some of the EDW team used Innovation Time for work related book clubs.

There are only two rules for Innovation Time:
1. How the time is invested must be transparent and included on team and tribe visualisations.
2. No one can "steal" your Innovation Time.

Rule number two was the result of some cheeky project managers, trying to get teams to work on additional projects by negotiating for the team to give up their Innovation Time!

While carving out time is generally a significant enabler to innovation, sometimes the tribe might need a little nudge to get started. For many, this may be the first time they have been given this degree of autonomy at work.

When we introduced Innovation Time at EDW it was accompanied by "The Innovation Challenge". The challenge was run every Sprint. Teams would enter the challenge by creating an innovation (something that improved the way the tribe worked) and posting a one-page explanation on the noticeboard in the kitchen. Teams were so competitive that they would keep their innovations a secret until the very last minute. I would go home on Wednesday nights and the notice board would be empty; when I arrived back in the office on Thursday morning, the "innovation fairies" had visited in the night and the board was filled with ideas.

---

[77] Bharat Mediratta and Julie Bick, "The Google Way: Give Engineers Room," *The New York Times*, October 21, 2007, accessed September 10, 2016, http://www.nytimes.com/2007/10/21/jobs/21pre.html?_r=0.

The teams would get to share their innovations with the rest of the tribe at Unity Hour and the tribe would vote for the most useful innovation. In the early days the winning team was given $100 to spend on whatever they liked. We expected they would probably use the money to buy themselves a round of drinks at the pub or something. Instead, they surprised us. They went to the local supermarket, bought chips and lollies,[78] then sent an email to the entire tribe saying: "Snacks at our place! Come and visit and learn about our innovation."

Later we dropped the cash prize and introduced the innovation cup. Interestingly, the teams were so much more competitive over the cup than they ever were over the money. Must have been that intrinsic motivation thing Daniel Pink was going on about!

So what has this got to do with connecting to a leader? Well, someone has to fight the good fight to create the time and fund the cup!

---

[78] For the Americans that is chips and candy! And for the Brits that is crisps and sweets!

Show Your Vulnerability

The vulnerability paradox: It's the first thing
I look for in you and the last thing I want you to see in me
—Brené Brown.

Perhaps the most powerful thing a leader can do to connect with their tribe is to show their soft underbelly. As leaders we ask our teams to be transparent and consequently vulnerable every day. It is only fair that we do the same as leadership teams. Our teams want to trust us; they are looking for vulnerability, proof we are human. It is incumbent on us as leaders to take the first step, show our vulnerability to our teams and give them the safety to reciprocate.

I don't ask this of you lightly. Personally I am extremely introverted and shy, which I can tell you is an utterly painful combination. In the early days of the EDW tribe Mark took great pleasure in setting me up to be horribly embarrassed and vulnerable in front of my tribe. On one occasion he made me participate in a learning activity that involved small teams throwing and catching tennis balls. Much to everyone's delight, hand-eye coordination is not one of my strengths, so I spent most of the game dropping tennis balls, laughing nervously, and turning very red. I think it would be fair to say I was most embarrassed.

When I reflected back on this experience, I recognised that while I was VERY uncomfortable during it, it was also very powerful in breaking down those invisible walls that exist between leaders and their teams. Inspired, I decided to share this story on my blog. Oh boy, would that turn out to be a mistake!

About a year later the EDW tribe decided to perform the Macarena in an attempt to win a corporate competition. They were hoping to win a shopping voucher that they would then use to buy themselves a PlayStation.

They needed the event recorded in order to enter the event, so my lieutenant and I decided to "take one for the team" and excuse ourselves from the dancing in order to capture both video and photographs of the event.

At the next Bubble Up one of the teams raised an issue that "Em did not do the Macarena". I went around and visited the team with the complaint and explained that I did not know how to do the Macarena to which one of them responded, "I read this blog once about *Leading through Vulnerability* …"[79] So I made them a deal. I would do the "Bus Stop"[80] next Unity Hour. Feeling that it was important that everyone suffered with me, I was accompanied by my leadership team. The result was an appalling attempt at the Bus Stop, a wonderful display of vulnerability, and a happy tribe.

Taking the Radical Leap

Do what you love in the service of people who love what you do
—Steve Farber, *The Radical Leap*.

The leadership framework that I have found to be most congruent with Tribal Unity is Steve Farber's Extreme Leadership Framework.[81] While I was not at all familiar with Steve's work when I started working with tribes, I have come to recognise that I had unwittingly taken the Radical LEAP.

---

[79] See: http://www.prettyagile.com/2013/07/leading-through-vulnerability.html

[80] In Australia, during the 80s and 90s, The Bus Stop was a well-known group dance that we did at school discos to the Fatback Band's *(Are you Ready) Do The Bus Stop*. I would put it in the same category as dances like the Nutbush and the Macarena.
See: https://www.youtube.com/watch?v=PeeOPR8bxac

[81] Steve Farber, *The Radical Leap: A Personal Lesson in Extreme Leadership*, (Poway: Mission Boulevard Press and Digital, 2014).

LEAP stands for Love, Energy, Audacity, and Proof.

Extreme Leaders:
Cultivate Love,
Generate Energy,
Inspire Audacity, and;
Provide Proof.

When I think back on my time leading the EDW tribe, there is not a shadow of doubt in my mind that despite all the ups and downs, I truly loved being part of that team. I believe that this was obvious to anyone who came into contact with me during that period of my life. I was fiercely protective of my tribe and fought tooth and nail on more than one occasion to keep the tribe intact. When I left, the tribe made a short feature film for me as a going-away gift. I remember sharing this with a friend at the time and her commenting on the love that radiated from the film. The team were kind enough to let me post it on my blog,[82] should you wish to judge for yourself.

When I think about tribal energy I can't help but make the association to Unity Hour and Cocktail Hour. Both rituals played a huge part in generating energy across the tribe. In terms of audacity, let's be frank, what on earth was a business person doing taking on the leadership of a technology team! And it's not like I was just keeping the seat warm. I took it upon myself to introduce a new methodology that I had read about in a book! In hindsight, I'm not sure if it was audacity or stupidity, but either way I got really lucky as the result was nothing short of amazing. There it is: the proof that it was all worthwhile.

---

[82] See: http://www.prettyagile.com/2014/05/time-to-catch-another-train.html

Chapter Summary

In this chapter we explored techniques for connecting tribes to their leaders.

- Successful tribe leaders need to participate in the change they are leading.
- The tribe leader has a moral responsibility to provide their tribe with the training and coaching to enable the tribe to understand and adopt new ways of working.
- Leaders can create connections with the people in their tribe by spending time at the gemba.
- It is the role of the tribe leader to improve the "system of work" for the people who do the work, i.e. their tribe. To do this the leader needs to "learn to see" how the work works.
- Leadership is a team sport. Every leader needs a strong team of lieutenants to aid them in serving the tribe.
- Leadership teams should use the same Minimal Viable Agility practices as the other teams in the tribe.
- It is incumbent upon the tribe's leader to provide the tribe with the time and space to innovate. An Innovation Challenge supported by Innovation Time is one technique for achieving this.
- Tribes thrive in safe environments. Leaders who are vulnerable and transparent with their tribes create the conditions in which their tribe feels safe.
- Extreme Tribe Leaders take the Radical LEAP: cultivate Love, generate Energy, inspire Audacity, and provide Proof.

As a friend of mine always says, "The fish rots from the head". The behaviour of the tribe's leader always dictates the tribe's culture. Is your behaviour lifting the culture of your tribe?

In the next section we will look at what it takes to connect the tribe to an idea.

PART 4

CONNECTING TO AN IDEA

True leadership inspires people with vision. Vision pulls people not only to take action but also to care about the outcome, to take personal ownership of it, and to bring their "A game" every day
—Christine Comaford, *Smart Tribes.*

Your tribe needs an idea to rally around, as Seth Godin says "something to believe in", "your vision and your passion".[83] In my view, it does not need to be as grand as Martin Luther King's "I have a dream" or JFK's mission to put a man on the moon. It must, however, be clear and it must be communicated.

In John Kotter's *Leading Change,* he highlights eight of the most common mistakes made by those leading change. Three of those concern the vision: "Underestimating the Power of Vision", "Under Communicating the Vision by a Factor of 10 (or 100 or Even 1000)", and "Permitting Obstacles to Block the Vision". [84] Kotter also tells us that an effective vision is: Imaginable, Desirable, Feasible, Focused, Flexible, and Communicable.[85]

When I launched the EDW Agile Release Train, my idea was simple. I wanted to move from a world of disparate project teams, all working to their own project visions, beating to the sound of their own drum and struggling to deliver, into an Agile Release Train, a successful team of Agile teams, that could deliver all the organisation's Enterprise Data Warehousing needs.

I communicated this vision to everyone and anyone. I was so excited! I'm told the passion I had for this vision radiated from me on a daily basis.

---

[83] Seth Godin. *Tribes,* location 73-116.

[84] John P. Kotter, *Leading Change,* (Boston: Harvard Business Review Press, 2012), Kindle Edition, Chapter 1.

[85] John P. Kotter, *Leading Change,* location 979.

Achieving Alignment With Book Clubs

The more you read, the more things you will know. The more you learn, the more places you'll go—Dr. Seuss.

The first people I told about my big idea—the EDW Agile Release Train—were my new leadership team. I arranged a series of workshops to pitch the idea of forming an Agile Release Train to my new team. From these workshops I hoped to achieve shared understanding and agreement on the shape of our future organisation. We kicked off with Mark Richards sharing what he had learned about Agile Release Trains from a workshop he had attended with Dean Leffingwell (the author of *Scaling Software Agility*, the book that gave us the idea in the first place). We also provided everyone with the details of Leffingwell's more recent book, *Agile Software Requirements*.

Through the workshops we debated various organisational models, operating principles, and approaches to getting started until we landed on a majority consensus on the way forward. With our vision agreed it was all hands on deck to get ready for our first PI Planning event tentatively scheduled to happen in about six weeks' time.

As the day of the event grew closer, I noticed that there were some blank faces among my extended leadership team when I referred to various aspects of what we needed to do. My heart sank as I asked the team, "Who has read the book?" A couple of hands were raised. "Who has finished the book?" Only one hand. "Who doesn't own the book?" At least four or five hands were sheepishly raised. "Okay," I said. "Change of plan. We are all going to buy the book. If you cannot afford the book, let me know and I will arrange a book for you. Then we are going to read the book together. We are going to form a book club!"

For the next three months I met with my extended leadership team for an hour a week. Each week one member of the team led a discussion on a chapter or two. We would discuss the concepts covered, how they might apply to our situation, and agree on the ideas we wanted to implement. Book club was compulsory and if one team member had something more important to do then book club was rescheduled. Shared understanding and agreement was paramount if we were going to be successful.

Visitors to the EDW Release Train were often shocked when they heard that I called a mandatory weekly meeting to read a book. I was always quick to remind them that no one would hesitate to call a "business" meeting, so why wouldn't we want to make time for a meeting focused on learning ways to improve our "business"?

While the "Leffingwell Book Club" (as it was fondly referred to) created the shared understanding that I was eager to achieve, there were some unexpected but positive side effects. First, more book clubs spun up; our Scrum masters read Lyssa Adkins' *Coaching Agile Teams*, our technical leads read Ken Collier's *Agile Analytics*, the test leads read Lisa Crispin's *Agile Testing*, and one of the delivery teams chose to read Mary and Tom Poppendieck's *Lean Software Development: An Agile Toolkit*. Second, the foundations of what would become our Leadership Continuous Improvement Team emerged as we created a kanban wall to track all the ideas we wanted to implement.[86]

The third and most amazing side effect of the book club was how it enabled the formation of a team. My extended leadership team was made up of various leaders from the three groups that had been merged to create my new organisation. Leffingwell's book gave us safe material to debate (no pun intended!). No one needed to be worried about hurting someone else's feelings when offering an opinion on the material.

---

[86] See: http://www.prettyagile.com/2014/04/being-agile-team-of-agile-leaders.html

Reading became a huge part of our learning culture. Who is reading what was a constant topic of conversation. When people visited us for "tours" the book club wall was one of the most photographed and talked about aspects of the EDW Agile Release Train. Some of our visitors have even been inspired to launched their own book clubs—and not just the Agile folk!

A year down the track our vision changed. We were now one team, a Stage Four tribe. It was time to step it up a notch. Our new vision was to become: World Leaders in Agile Data Warehousing. And as you already know, we had that printed on our tribe T-shirts! While I'm not sure we ever attained "World Leader" status we did get a very nice compliment on the blog of Agile Data Warehousing guru, Ken Collier: *"This is probably the most well-scaled agile data warehousing group I've ever observed, and they are still getting better."*[87]

---

[87] See: http://theagilist.com/2013/09/03/scaling-agile-data-warehousing/

All you really need to create the vision for your tribe is some inspiration. Inspiration can come from anywhere. A number of tribes I have had the privilege of working with have taken their inspiration from the EDW tribe. Others are more market driven and are striving to position their organisation as best in class. Given you are reading this book maybe your vision is as straightforward as mine was: Tribal Unity and a One Team Culture.

Communicating the Vision

A vision statement doesn't generate energy, love does, great ideas do, principles and values do. A vision statement that comes from a workshop exercise is usually about as energising and memorable as a saltine cracker
—Steve Farber, *The Radical Leap.*

No matter how many times you communicate your vision it will never be enough. Employees in this day and age are bombarded with communications and no message will stick every time. Many years ago I worked with a change manager who told me you need to hear a message seven times before you will remember it. I have no idea of his source, but when I think about the challenges of communicating to a tribe, I believe him.

If you are holding Unity Hours and Tribe Syncs then you have two easily accessible forums in which to keep repeating the messages. Guerrilla marketing is my friend Wayne's favourite technique. This would tend to manifest itself as posters on the walls in the men's bathrooms. When it comes to sticky communication techniques that one nicely ticks the box of "unexpected".[88]

---

[88] Chip Heath and Dan Heath, *Made to Stick: Why Some Ideas Survive and Others Die*, (New York: Random House, 2007) Kindle Edition.

It is also important that you are congruent in the way you deliver this message. I was reminded of this recently when watching Vinh Giang's TEDx video, *Creating the most influential you*.[89] Vinh is a magician and he shares with the audience the importance of sight, sound, and sync when it comes to showmanship and presentation. The bit that stuck with me was sync: if the magician's actions are incongruent with his words then we don't believe him and the magic doesn't work. The same is true for any communication effort.

A SAFe style PI Planning event can be helpful here too. These events always open with messages from senior executives communicating their vision. I love these moments. There is nothing quite like watching a tribe hear from their CEO, CIO, CFO, or other CxO, how their works connects to the organisation's mission. It is nothing short of inspiring. You may have heard the story of President John F. Kennedy visiting the NASA space centre and asking a janitor what his role was. The janitor's reply: *"I'm helping to put a man on the moon."* This is your tribe's man on the moon moment.

Dealing With Detractors

The art of leadership is understanding what you can't compromise on
—Seth Godin, *Tribes.*

There are always going to be people who don't get on board with where you want to go. It is inevitable. Some of them will be in your tribe; some of them will be from outside your tribe. Time and proof is usually the best remedy. You need time to turn your vision into action and time for your action to deliver results. Most people will give you six months and in my experience that is more than enough time to prove that your trajectory is positive.

---

[89] See: http://tedxtalks.ted.com/video/Creating-the-most-influential-y

Some people might leave. While it doesn't happen often, it does happen. In my experience it will be less than 5% of your workforce. In fact, one of the great advantages of Tribal Unity is that your employee retention is likely to be off the charts.

When it comes to detractors from outside your organisation, the serenity prayer[90] will probably come in handy! Some of them will experience working with your tribe and get on board, others will always find an excuse for why your success isn't real.

Strong leadership is really important here. Stay true to what you believe in. Be cautious about where and how you compromise. My advice: stick to your guns, build an incredible tribe, and tell the world about it.

Stay True to Your Idea

Good is the enemy of great
—Jim Collins, *Good to Great.*

Sometimes your lack of confidence can be your biggest detractor. Just like Kevin Costner in *Field of Dreams*[91] you need to believe in your idea if you are going to succeed. Making bold, sweeping change based on an idea you read about in a book is scary. I know this. I have been there. Whatever you do, do not lose your nerve.

When leaders compromise on their vision for their organisation there is a risk that they will fall into the trap of settling for "good enough" rather than striving for great. Now I am not by any means advocating

---

[90] *"God, grant me the serenity to accept the things I cannot change, Courage to change the things I can, And wisdom to know the difference"* https://en.wikipedia.org/wiki/Serenity_Prayer

[91] See: http://www.imdb.com/title/tt0097351/

perfection, as this has its own limitations, but rather I am suggesting you be cautious in how far you stray from your original intent. A pattern I have seen a lot is people who scale back their idea to something more palatable, achieve a good result, but then never go on to implement the full idea, subsequently falling short of the potential greatness.

In organisations implementing SAFe, there are often nerves about scheduling the first PI Planning Event. The thought of putting one hundred plus team members in the same room as your most important stakeholders for two days for a "workshop" can be utterly terrifying. Some people deal with this by compromising and doing something a little less bold. Generally, whatever path they choose delivers a good result. So they reach the conclusion that they were right to compromise, unwittingly settling for good over great. In the end, it's all a matter of perspective. How can you be great if you don't know what great looks like?

On the other end of the spectrum is the group of people who lack the confidence to execute their full idea, scale it back, implement, fail, then blame the idea. There is this great blog post by Ron Jeffries[92] called *We Tried Baseball and It Didn't Work*[93] that illustrates this perfectly. In this post Jeffries tells what I assume is a fictional account of a team that decided that many of the rules of baseball are "stupid" and therefore they decide to change things like the number of players, the number of bases, the size of the field, the specifications for the bat and ball, and so on. Lo and behold, when they play the "improved" game they discover it is "no fun at all". Leading them to conclude that: *"We tried baseball, and it didn't work."*

---

[92] Ron Jeffries is one of the three founders of the Extreme Programming (XP) software development methodology along with Kent Beck and Ward Cunningham. XP is one of several methods included in the umbrella term Agile. https://en.wikipedia.org/wiki/Ron_Jeffries

[93] See: http://ronjeffries.com/xprog/articles/jatbaseball/

Chapter Summary

In this chapter we explored techniques for helping the tribe connect with an idea.

- Sharing your ideas for the future with your tribe gives them something to believe in and rally behind.
- Your idea doesn't have to be grand, it can be as simple as Tribal Unity and a One Team Culture.
- No matter how many times you think you have repeated, reinforced, and shared your vision of the future with your tribe you have most likely under communicated it.
- Communication practices like book clubs, Unity Hour and Cocktail Hour can be leveraged to help you increase the awareness of your vision across the tribe.
- The best approach for tackling detractors is to dazzle them with success.
- You need to fully believe in and commit to your idea if you want to achieve great results.

Every tribe needs a mission in the same way every team does. This mission, or idea, provides alignment and helps the tribe pull together in times of crises. You cannot achieve Tribal Unity if everyone is heading in different directions.

In the next section we will explore approaches to sustaining Tribal Unity.

PART 5

SUSTAINING TRIBAL UNITY

...change sticks only when it becomes "the way we do things around here", when it seeps into the very bloodstream of the work unit...
—John Kotter, *Leading Change.*

So you have done it: you have created your tribe, you have connected a group to one another, to a leader, and an idea! Woo hoo! Congratulations. Party time!

Wait! Come back here! Before you rush off to the party, remember Kotter and his eight common mistakes? Well, you are about to make number eight: "Neglecting to Anchor the Changes Firmly in the Corporate Culture".[94] So, how are you going to keep the momentum going?

Quantifying Culture With the Net Promoter System

Businesses often forget about the culture, and ultimately,
they suffer for it because you can't deliver good service from unhappy employees
—Tony Hsieh, CEO, Zappos.

It seems that most companies have some sort of annual Employee Engagement Survey. I know every large corporate I have ever worked for has something of this nature. My experience with these surveys tells me that they are not overly useful. Once a year the organisation sends out a link to an online survey. The survey only goes to permanent staff because clearly contractors and consultants aren't real people. (You knew that, right?) There are in the vicinity of 70 questions asked on a 7-point scale. Approximately three months after the survey is taken, managers who have more than 10 responses for their group get sent a rather large PowerPoint report and get told to "fix it". Personally, I never worked out how to make that work. Instead, I found something called the Net Promoter System (NPS).

---

[94] John Kotter, *Leading Change*, location 245.

For those of you not familiar with NPS it is a customer loyalty metric, developed by Fred Reichheld and Bain & Co. NPS is measured by "the ultimate question": "On a Scale from 0 to 10, where 0 is not at all likely and 10 is extremely likely, how likely are you to recommend [Company Name] to a friend or colleague?" Responses are categorised into Promoters (scores of 9 and 10), Passives (scores of 7 and 8) and Detractors (scores of 6 or less). The percentage of promoters minus the percentage of detractors is the Net Promoter Score. The logic being that the 9's and 10's are statistically likely to actually recommend your product and those that score 6 and below are likely to say something negative. The analytics that underpins all of this is spelt out in Reichheld's book *The Ultimate Question 2.0.*[95]

What has all of this got to do with employee engagement? One of the findings in *The Ultimate Question 2.0* is: *"You can't create loyal customers without first creating loyal employees."*[96] Or as I like to phrase it: "Happy teams lead to happy customers". The book goes on to recommend implementing an employee NPS (eNPS) process that asks: "On a scale of 0 to 10, how likely is it you would recommend this company as a place to work?" followed by an open-ended question like: "What are the primary reasons for your score?" In my view this is the perfect metric with which to measure Tribal Unity. All you need is a Survey Monkey account and you are in business!

My approach is usually to set up a three-question survey that I send out once a quarter. It should take no more than two minutes to complete and you should be able to get close to 100% response within a week (with a little nagging).

---

[95] Fred Reichheld, *The Ultimate Question 2.0: How Net Promoter Companies Thrive in a Customer-Driven World*, (Boston: Harvard Business Review Press, 2011).

[96] Fred Reichheld, *The Ultimate Question 2.0*, p165.

Sample Tribe eNPS Survey

This short survey is designed to understand your experience working in the [TRIBE NAME].

By default, your responses are completely anonymous. You can choose to provide your name at the end of the survey.

1. On a scale of 0 to 10, where 0 is not at all likely and 10 is extremely likely, how likely is it you would recommend [TRIBE NAME] as a place to work?

[If 9 or 10]
2. What is the PRIMARY reason you would recommend working in [TRIBE NAME]?

[If 7 or 8]
3. What is the MOST important thing that the [TRIBE NAME] needs to change for you to give a score of 9 or 10?

[If 6 or below]
4. What is the PRIMARY reason you would not recommend working in the [TRIBE NAME]?

5. What other comments would you like to share about your experience working in the [TRIBE NAME]?

6. Your name (optional)

Thank you for completing this survey

The value in eNPS is not so much the numerical score as it is the feedback to the open-ended questions. The feedback can be very confronting and other times exceedingly pleasing. The key is to learn from it and take action where required. And, yes, I can confirm, in my experience happy teams do lead to happy customers!

Record and Share Your Tribal Stories

Maybe stories are just data with a soul
—Brené Brown.

Throughout human history, tribes have used storytelling to pass their history from one generation to the next. In the modern age we have many more tools at our disposal for story telling that there is just no excuse not to.

As you create your tribe, remember to take photos and videos to capture those memories for your tribe today and its future generations: go old school and print some photos every so often and put them up in the office; create walls filled with memories of past Unity Hours and Breakaway Days.

Invite people to visit your tribe and learn about your success. People from all over Australia and even some international folks visited the EDW tribe. We would take them on tours of our workspace, invite them to witness Unity Hour or Cocktail Hour, and share with them the story of how the EDW Release Train came to be.

I ran tours a couple of times a month. I had a standard one-hour tour schedule that would start at a wall with a large poster of the SAFe Big Picture, where I would share the back story of why we chose to implement SAFe and specifically how we had chosen to interpret it. I would then take the tourists on a walk of the walls, showing them how work flows through the train. Visitors would always stop and ask questions about the artefacts on our walls, photos of past Unity Hours, our book club wall, images from Breakaway Day. Each artefact contained one of our tribal legends that I would then share with the tour group.

My blog[97] also became a way that the EDW tribal stories were recorded. People were forever charging into my office to tell me about their latest experiment only to ask if I would blog about it. This pattern has continued as I have worked with other tribes. They always ask: "When are you going to blog about us?" These stories and blogs also support the proof element of Extreme Leadership that we talked about in Part 4.

Sustained Greatness Requires Discipline

We've found in all our research studies that the signature of
mediocrity is not an unwillingness to change; the
signature of mediocrity is chronic inconsistency
—Jim Collins, *Great by Choice*.

Staying the course is not easy, especially as your tribe begins to gain momentum. It is so easy to get fooled into thinking that your work is done. It takes time and repetition for change to stick. The good news is it can be done. At the time of writing the EDW tribe has been humming along for over four years. They still hold Unity Hour every two weeks and Cocktail Hour every morning.

There will be times when the tribe tries to tell you they are "too busy" for Unity Hour, or some other tribe ritual. Don't let them off the hook. I recently heard a story about a tribe that had implemented Scrum. Over the first six months the tribe had complained that there

---

[97] See: www.prettyagile.com

were too many meetings.[98] Eventually the leadership succumbed to the pressure from the tribe and scaled back the meetings. Unfortunately, the end result was that the momentum the tribe had achieved began to slowly decay. I have seen similar things happen to teams and tribes that stop doing retrospectives or cease to invest in the sort of tribal kaizen activities that we talked about in Part 2.

Being disciplined also means being consistent. While we experimented a lot at EDW, we placed the utmost importance on providing consistent messages to the tribe. Our experiments were always congruent with our vision of becoming "World Leaders in Agile Data Warehousing".

At EDW, being consistent with our values sometimes meant I had to face some tough conversations with the broader organisation when they made demands on my team that were not consistent with our values. For example, as Agile practitioners we subscribed to the principle of sustainable pace, so when it was suggested to us that we ask our tribe to work multiple weekends in a row, the answer had to be no. Consistency is not easy but it is a discipline you need to master if you are going to sustain Tribal Unity.

---

[98] Most Scrum implementation will have the following meetings:
- Sprint Planning: a four-hour time-boxed planning meeting at the beginning of a two-week Sprint
- Daily Scrum: a daily 15-minute stand-up meeting
- Sprint review: a one-to-two-hour review of the work completed during the Sprint with a particular focus demonstrating what is done
- Sprint retrospective: a one-hour retrospective like the ones we looked at in Part 1

Many Scrum teams also have at least one two-hour backlog refinement meeting each Sprint and at scale there may also be Scrum of Scrums meetings two or three times a week.

Setting Up Successors for Success

We say at Toyota that every leader is a teacher developing the next generation of leaders
—Akio Toyoda.

When I left the EDW tribe, I had complete faith in the team I left behind. But I still was concerned that the organisation would close in on them. After all, the transformation that took place within the EDW tribe was mostly unique and not replicated across the corporation. I did have some reasons to be hopeful, as over the years I had observed that the "bright spot" that was the EDW tribe had inspired change in other parts of the organisation. For example, some groups across the broader department had started their own Unity Hour, the practice of using eNPS had been adopted by various teams across the organisation, and more Agile Release Trains had been launched in other lines of business.

In the management classic, *Good to Great*, Jim Collins and his team identified seven concepts that were present in companies that had made the leap from good to great. One of the seven was the concept of "Level 5 Leadership".[99] That is, leaders who display the following behavioural patterns:
- Setting up successors for success
- A compelling modesty
- Unwavering resolve ... to do what must be done
- The Window and the Mirror[100]

---

[99] Jim Collins, *Good to Great: Why Some Companies Make the Leap...and Others Don't*, (New York: HarperCollins, 2001)

[100] *"Level 5 leaders look out the window to apportion credit to factors outside themselves when things go well (and if they cannot find a specific person or event to give credit to, they credit good luck). At the same time, they look in the mirror to apportion responsibility, never blaming bad luck when things go poorly."* Collins, *Good to Great*, p35.

When it comes to sustaining Tribal Unity, you need to ensure that the tribe's longevity isn't tied to your tenure leading them. It is up to you to ensure that the improvements you champion are sustainable. There is nothing more disheartening for the teams you work with to be led to a better place only to find it is an illusion.

Chapter Summary

In this chapter we explored techniques for sustaining Tribal Unity.

- Monitor the health of your tribe using the employee Net Promoter System (eNPS). Don't forget to action the feedback in order to maintain and improve your tribe's culture.
- Use storytelling to remind your tribe of where it came from and reinforce your tribe's values.
- Be disciplined about your tribe's rituals and values. Over time complacency will lead to the disintegration of Tribal Unity.
- Remember to develop a team of leaders that can fill your shoes when you move to your next tribe. The greatest compliment to your leadership is a tribe with self-sustaining Tribal Unity.

Being prepared to sustain Tribal Unity is core to the mindset that a tribe leader needs to succeed with Tribal Unity. Just like a garden, your tribe needs to be cared for and maintained if it is to continue to grow in a healthy manner.

The next section is for those who need help getting their management to buy in to implementing Tribal Unity. If this is not a challenge you are facing you may like to skip ahead to the conclusion.

PART 6

ENGAGING MANAGEMENT IN TRIBAL UNITY

One of the things that limits our learning is our belief that we already know something—L. David Marquet, *Turn the Ship Around!*

The number one question I get asked when I talk about Tribal Unity is: "how do I get my management to buy into this?" The intent of this chapter is to provide you with some tools to help unlock your leader's intrinsic motivation.

Before we launch into how we might inspire your leader to behave differently, I'm curious as to why you think they would not like to achieve Tribal Unity? I find many people are quick to see management as a blocker to progressing new ways of working. It can be useful to remember that managers are people too. Just like everyone else, they come to work every day with the intention of doing a good job.

I'm reminded of researcher Brené Brown's book *Rising Strong* in which she explores the concept of the stories we tell ourselves in order to make sense of the world around us. Often these stories are inaccurate and incomplete. Brown challenges her readers to reality check these stories.[101] Take a moment now to write down the story you are telling yourself about your experiences with your management. Then step back and consider if it is possible that there is a delta between the story you are telling yourself and the truth of the situation. *"What is the most generous assumption you can make about this person's intentions or what this person said?"*[102]

Many years ago I was given some really good advice, that I can't claim I always follow: assume good intent. If you can do this, then you are well placed to help your management get inspired to achieve Tribal Unity.

---

[101] Brené Brown, *Rising Strong*, (London: Vermilion, 2015), Kindle Edition.

[102] Brené Brown, *Rising Strong*, location 1635.

Tap Into Your Empathy

*Empathy is connection with the emotion
that someone is experiencing...*
—Brené Brown, *Daring Greatly*.

Now we have assumed good intent, we are in a good place to try and gain an appreciation of what is going on for your management. My suggestion is that you start by trying to put yourself in your manager's shoes.

A tool you may find useful in the process is Empathy Mapping, originally intended as a way to quickly create a customer or user profile,[103] I have also found it useful for creating perspective in the workplace. All you need to do is draw out a map, like the one below,[104] and then ask yourself what is going on right now for your manager. What are

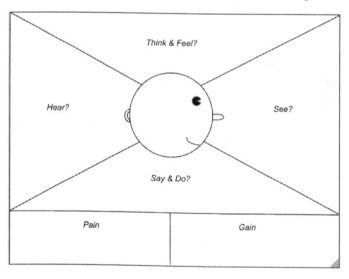

---

[103] David Gray, Sunni Brown, and James Macanufo, *Gamestorming: A Play book for Innovators, Rulebreakers, and Changemakers*, (Sebastopol: O'Reilly, 2010), Kindle Edition, location 1124.

[104] Source: http://www.solutionsiq.com/what-is-an-empathy-map/

they thinking, feeling, seeing, saying, doing, and hearing? And perhaps most importantly in this context, what is causing them pain and what do they stand to gain from Tribal Unity?

Depending on your circumstances you may like to do this as a collaborative activity with some of your peers. The goal is to identify a way to connect your leader to the idea of Tribal Unity. Can you influence what is going on around them? What they are seeing or hearing or even doing? Would Tribal Unity address some pain they are feeling? These are the opportunities we are looking for.

Help Your Leaders Learn

Those who can read and don't are only marginally better off than those who can't
—Verne Harnish.

One approach to influencing what your management is thinking is by encouraging them to read. Many managers don't read or if they do, perhaps they are not reading the right things. Personally I have always been an avid reader of fiction with the odd business book thrown in here and there. When I first became interested in Agile and Lean, I was encouraged to turn my attention to books more relevant to what we were trying to achieve with the EDW tribe. My first serious read was Jim Highsmith's *Agile Project Management*. This turned out to be a great enabler for me. It put me in a position to ask questions about what was going on around me, such as why do we have 23 people in an Agile team?

Today I still read a lot but I rarely read fiction. While I still enjoy fiction when I get around to reading it, my thirst for knowledge has become unquenchable. There is just no substitute for self-education.

If your management aren't readers perhaps consider a book club, like the one I ran with my leadership team at EDW, or perhaps recommend something you have read. Both approaches will open up the opportunity for discussion and debate about how some new ideas might be able to be applied in your context. Of course, recommending this book would be a great choice! However, here are some other suggestions, in no particular order:

Tribal Leadership, David Logan
The Radical Leap, Steve Farber
Leading Teams, J. Richard Hackman
Turn the Ship Around! L. David Marquet
Smart Tribes, Christine Comaford
Good to Great, Jim Collins
Great by Choice, Jim Collins
Switch, Chip and Dan Heath
Managing for Happiness, Jurgen Appelo
The Toyota Way to Lean Leadership, Jeffrey Liker
Joy Inc., Richard Sheridan

If you cannot get traction with the reading do not give up. Remember, managers are human and that means just like the rest of us they don't know what they don't know. If we want to influence their thinking, we have to introduce new concepts.

Perhaps your management would respond better to something a little less academic. Is there a local Meetup[105] group they could join that would expose them to different ways of thinking? Maybe this is something you could do together as a leadership group. Conferences can also be excellent sources of inspiration. You could also consider reaching out to leaders in your local community who might be willing to chat with your management about their experiences. I know over the

---

[105] See: https://www.meetup.com/

years I have I had a constant stream of requests to talk to other leaders about my experiences with Tribal Unity.

Shine a Light on a Bright Spot

...search the community for bright spots—successful efforts worth emulating
—Chip and Dan Heath, *Switch*.

In their book, *Switch: How to Change Things When Change is Hard*, Chip and Dan Heath talk about change using the analogy of the Elephant and the Rider, where the Elephant is our emotional side and the Rider is our rational side. If the Elephant doesn't want to go in the direction of the Rider, then the Rider is outmatched and the Elephant goes the way it wants. For a change to be effective, the Heath brothers suggest you need to:

- Direct the Rider
- Motivate the Elephant
- And Shape the Path[106]

A technique that tends to appeal to both the rational and emotional side of leaders is site visits to "bright spots". That is, find relevant examples of a great tribe that has been enabled by their management and shine a light on it. "Bright spots" appeal to the rider as it provides proof of what is possible while also appealing to the elephant as the leader gets to experience what Tribal Unity feels like for themselves.

For example, one of the services I used to offer to the broader company and the local IT community was running tours of the EDW Agile Release Train. We had a constant stream of people wanting to bring their management to our "Unity Day" event and to "walk the walls". I think the thank-you note I received from one coach who brought his

---

[106] Chip Heath and Dan Heath, *Switch*, location 125.

leadership team through is a perfect illustration of how shining a light on the bright spots can work: *"Thanks for today. It was great to see how far you and the EDW team have come. It has really helped to enforce the Agile change ideas within my [Department's] leadership group and show them what is truly possible if you put your mind to it ☺ "*

Invite Your Leaders to the Gemba

The only way we can really understand
problems is at the Gemba
—Aiko Toyoda.

Remember that invisible wall between the leader and teams that we talked about in Part 3? When it comes to breaking through that wall what is stopping you from jumping over it and offering an olive branch? If we assume good intent, then odds are your management thinks that they are doing the right thing by not intruding in your space.

Invite your management to the gemba and change what they are seeing and hearing. I don't mean send them an Outlook meeting request, I mean go and talk to them: stick your head in their office or ambush them in the tea room, whatever works. Be clear about what you are asking for, then make the request. You could invite them to join a team meeting, ask them to participate in a Lean Coffee session with your team, or ask them to visit your team wall so you can show them some challenges you are having that they might be able to help with. Managers can be exceptionally good at following simple instructions; such as, "Can you please call x and ask them to approve y?" or "I need you to send an email to x about y today. I have drafted this for you and it is in your inbox".

Suggest One Small Change

What is the simplest thing that could possibly work?
—Kent Beck, *Extreme Programming Explained.*

When I am working with leaders in organisations that are unsure about making a revolutionary change, I like to start with something small but impactful. The idea is to choose a concept that you are almost certain will work: get agreement to make that one small change, implement it, and be phenomenally successful. Now you have a ticket to play! Find the next small thing that you are confident will work and rinse and repeat.

To increase the likelihood the manager will act on your suggestion, make it easy for them to do so. Managers are always time poor; the more pieces you put into place for them, the more likely they are to go along with your idea.

Chapter Summary

In this section we explored techniques for engaging your management in Tribal Unity.

- Assume good intent.
- Look at the world from your manager's perspective and identify opportunities to change their perspective or address their pain. Empathy Mapping can be a useful tool for this.
- Books are an excellent source of self-education and inspiration for leaders.
- Exposing your management to "bright spots" will help with them both rationally and emotionally buying into Tribal Unity.
- Remember your management may not feel welcome at the gemba so it is up to you to invite them in so that they can get a broader perspective and recognise the need for Tribal Unity.
- Start with one small change you are confident will make a difference and use this success to build your management's confidence in adopting Tribal Unity.

Never forget your management is human and therefore they are likely to find change uncomfortable, If you aspire to Tribal Unity, take the lead and guide your management. To lead change you don't need a fancy title, you just need to dig deep and have the courage to take the first step.

CONCLUSION

Unless someone like you
cares a whole awful lot,
nothing is going to get better.
It's not.
—Dr Seuss, *The Lorax.*

Achieving Tribal Unity isn't hard. (Don't you just love how I made you read the whole book before revealing that little tidbit?) At its core it is about creating an environment where people feel safe to be themselves at work. Now I know at least some of you are thinking: of course this works when your workplace is full of whacky Australians. I promise you this is not a whacky Aussie thing; most of the tribes I work with are made up of people from all walks of life and many of them are not Aussies.

The time I spent leading the EDW tribe was one of the most incredible experiences of my life. I worked with some truly extraordinary people who made every day fun (even when it was very challenging!) and I will be forever grateful for the opportunity I was given, as a business person, to lead and grow a struggling delivery team into a world-class Agile Release Train.

As the general manager responsible for the launch of the EDW Release Train, I was invited to speak at conferences across Australia and the United States. I got to share our story and inspire others to take the next step in their journey to Tribal Unity. But the thing I treasure the most is the personal messages from the tribe. During the course of my last day various members of the team dropped by as I packed up my office.

"Thank you for making me agile."
"Thank you for changing what it is like to work here."
"Thank you for allowing me to be part of the journey."
"Thank you for the opportunity."
"Thank you for the experience."
"Good Luck, Em. Go and change the world!"

Their willingness to "drink the Kool-Aid" and come on the wild ride to launch Australia's first SAFe Agile Release Train is something I will never be able to thank them enough for. It was an absolute pleasure to work with such a dedicated, driven, and fun group of people. I can only hope that I am lucky enough to get an opportunity to work with such a great team again one day. This book is their legacy.

The secret to a great tribe is great leadership. The secret to great leadership is you. Anyone can do this. Take a deep breath, start where you are, then take the next logical step, inspect and adapt, then rinse and repeat, and you will be on your way.

My hope is that it has inspired you to make a change in your world.

Go forth and change some lives for the better!

APPENDIX

THE TRIBAL UNITY CHECKLIST

Create Great Teams

- Form cross-functional teams of seven ± two, with a shared mission.
- Use the self-selection approach to forming teams in order to kick-start your journey to Tribal Unity.
- Provide clear direction to the teams regarding the expectation that they adopt the Minimal Viable Agility practices:
    - Perform retrospectives on cadence
    - Physically visualise the team's work
    - Communicate daily about the team's priorities for the day ahead.
- Encourage teams to create social contracts and display them in their team space.
- Co-locate teams wherever possible.
- If distributed teams are unavoidable, then invest in the enabling technology to achieve virtual co-location.

Connect the Teams and Create a Tribe

- Create a shared identity for the tribe and the teams.
- Implement rituals such as Unity Hour and Cocktail Hour to provide frequent shared experiences across the tribe.
- Build a physical visualisation that summaries the work of the tribe.
- Use chapters to maintain the connection between specialists.
- Celebrate as a tribe (not as individual teams).
- Establish rituals such as the Bubble Up to foster Tribal Kaizen.
- Consider emulating the SAFe Quick-Start to accelerate the path to Tribal Unity.

Connect the Tribe to a Leader

- Be actively involved in the change.
- Ensure everyone in the tribe gets the training that they need to adopt the Minimal Viable Agility practices.

- Visit the tribe at the gemba and ask "How can I help?"
- Understand how the work works and then take steps to improve the system for the people who work in it.
- Identify your lieutenants and form a leadership team for your tribe.
- Have the tribe's leadership team adopt the same Minimal Viable Agility practices as the other teams in the tribe.
- Actively be of service to your tribe by actioning their requests for help.
- Create time and space for the tribe to innovate.
- Be vulnerable in front of your tribe. This builds trust.
- Become an Extreme Leader. Take the Radical Leap: cultivate Love, generate Energy, inspire Audacity, and provide Proof to your tribe that it has all been worthwhile.

Connect the Tribe to an Idea

- Have a vision for your tribe.
- Help your tribe understand your vision.
- Establish book clubs to spread your ideas.
- Communicate, communicate, and communicate your vision for the tribe.
- To silence detractors: focus on what is in your control and succeed.
- Be true to your original idea.

Sustaining Tribal Unity

- Monitor your tribe's health on a quarterly basis using the employee Net Promoter Score (eNPS).
- Action the eNPS feedback to maintain and improve your tribe's culture.
- Record and share your tribal legends.
- Be disciplined about continuing tribal rituals.
- Build the next generation of leaders for your tribe.

BIBLIOGRAPHY

Appelo, J., *Management 3.0: Leading Agile Developers, Developing Agile Leaders*, Boston: Pearson, 2011, PDF Edition.

Appelo, J., *#Workout, Games, Tools & Practices to Engage People, Improve Work, and Delight Clients*. Rotterdam: Happy Melly, 2014. Kindle Edition.

Appelo, J., *Managing for Happiness: Games, Tools, and Practices to Motivate Any Team*. New Jersey: Wiley, 2016. Kindle Edition.

Beck, K., *Extreme Programming Explained: Embrace Change 2nd Edition*, Boston: Pearson, 2004. Kindle Edition.

Brooks, Jr., F.P., The *Mythical Man-Month: Essays on Software Engineering, Anniversary Edition*, Addison-Wesley, 1995.

Cockburn, A., *Agile Software Development: The Cooperative Game*, Boston: Pearson, 2007. Kindle Edition.

Collier, K., *Agile Analytics: A Value-Driven Approach to Business Intelligence and Data Warehousing*, Pearson, 2012, Kindle Edition.

Collins, J., *Good to Great: Why Some Companies Make the Leap...and Others Don't*, New York: HarperCollins, 2001.

Collins, J. and M.T. Hansen, *Great by Choice: Uncertainly, Chaos and Luck – Why Some Thrive Despite Them All*, HarperCollins, 2011. Kindle Edition.

Comaford, C., *Smart Tribes: How Teams Become Brilliant Together*, London: Penguin, 2013. Kindle Edition.

Derby, E. and D. Larson, *Agile Retrospectives: Making Good Teams Great*. Raleigh: Pragmatic Bookshelf, 2005. Kindle Edition.

Farber, S., *The Radical Leap: A Personal Lesson in Extreme Leadership*, Poway: Mission Boulevard Press and Digital, 2014.

Godin, S., *Tribes: We Need You to Lead Us*. London: Hachette Digital, 2008. Kindle Edition.

Gray, D., S. Brown and J. Macanufo, *Gamestorming: A Play book for Innovators, Rulebreakers, and Changemakers,* Sebastopol: O'Reilly, 2010 Kindle Edition.

Hackman, J. R., *Leading Teams: Setting the Stage for Great Performances*. Boston: Harvard University Press, 2002. Kindle Edition.

Hackman, J. R., *Collaborative Intelligence: Using Teams to Solve Hard Problems* San Francisco: Berrett-Koehler, 2011. Kindle Edition.

Hammarberg, M. and J. Sundén, *Kanban in Action,* New York: Manning, 2014. PDF Edition.

Heath, C. and D. Heath, *Made to Stick: Why Some Ideas Survive and Others Die*, New York: Random House, 2007.

Heath, C. and D. Heath, *Switch: How to Change Things When Change is Hard*, London: Random House, 2010.

Highsmith, J., *Agile Project Management, Second Edition*, Boston: Pearson, 2010. Kindle Edition.

Hohmann, L., *Innovation Games: Creating Breakthrough Products Through Collaborative Play*, Boston: Pearson, 2007. Kindle Edition.

Kniberg, H., *Lean From the Trenches: Managing Large Scale Projects with Kanban*. Raleigh: Pragmatic Bookshelf, 2011.

Kotter, J.P., *Leading Change*. Boston: Harvard Business Review Press, 2012. Kindle Edition.

Leffingwell, D., *Scaling Software Agility: Best Practices for Large Enterprises*. Boston: Pearson, Boston, 2007. Kindle edition.

Leffingwell, D., *Agile Software Requirements: Lean Requirements Practices for Teams, Program, and the Enterprise*. Boston: Pearson, Boston, 2011. Kindle edition.

Lencioni, P., *The Five Dysfunctions of a Team: A Leadership Fable*, New York: Wiley, 2002. Kindle Edition.

Liker, J.K. and G.L. Convis, *The Toyota Way to Lean Leadership: Achieving and Sustaining Excellence Through Leadership Development*, McGraw-Hall, 2012. Kindle Edition.

Logan, D., J. King, and H. Fischer-Wright, *Tribal Leadership: How Successful Groups form Great Organizations*, HarperCollins, 2008. Kindle Edition.

Mamoli, S. and D. Mole, *Creating Great Teams: How Self-Selection Lets People Excel*. Raleigh: Pragmatic Bookshelf, 2015. PDF Edition.

Manns, M.L. and L. Rising, *Fearless Change: Patterns for Introducing New Ideas*, Boston: Pearson, 2005. Kindle Edition

Martin, K. and M. Osterling, *Value Stream Mapping: How to Visualize Work and Align Leadership for Organizational Transformation*. McGraw-Hill, 2014. Kindle Edition.

McChrystal, General Stanley et al., *Team of Teams: New Rules of Engagement for a Complex World*. New York: Penguin, 2015. Kindle Edition.

Moussa, M., M. Boyer, and D. Newberry, *Committed Teams: Three Steps to Inspiring Passion and Performance*, New Jersey: Wiley, 2016, Kindle Edition.

Pink, D.H., *Drive: The Surprising Truth About What Motivates Us*. New York: Riverhead Books, 2009.

Reichheld, F., *The Ultimate Question 2.0: How Net Promoter Companies Thrive in a Customer-Driven World*. Boston: Harvard Business Review Press, 2011.

Rother, M., *Toyota Kata: Managing People for Improvement, Adaptiveness, and Superior Results*, McGraw-Hill, 2010. Kindle Edition.

Sheridan, R., *Joy, Inc.: How We Built a Workplace People Love*. New York: Penguin, 2013. Kindle Edition.

Sutton, R.I. and H. Rao., *Scaling Up Excellence: Getting to More Without Settling for Less*, New York: Crown, 2014.

Thomas, K., *Get it On!: What It Means to Lead the Way*. Nashville: B&H, 2011.

Weinberg, G.M., *Why Software Gets in Trouble*, Software Quality Series: Vol. 2, Leanpub, 2016. PDF Edition.

About the Author

Em Campbell-Pretty

Scaled Agile Framework 4.0 Program Consultant Trainer (SPCT4)
Extreme Leadership Certified Facilitator

After close to 20 years in business management roles within multinational blue chip corporations, Em discovered Agile and became passionate about the opportunity it provides to align business and IT around the delivery of value. In 2012, she launched Australia's first Scaled Agile Framework (SAFe) Agile Release Train. The story of the cultural transformation that accompanied the launch of this train has become legendary in the Agile community, which has led to her being considered a thought leader on scaling Agile culture.

A true servant leader, Em is committed to building great teams and transforming culture whilst still maintaining focus on delivering business outcomes. At the heart of Em's success is her unrelenting focus on building a culture of transparency, Lean leadership, learning, and innovation.

Em is an active member of the global Agile community and was invited to co-chair the Enterprise Agile track for the Agile Alliance 2014, 2015, and 2016 conferences. She is a recognised expert in Scaling Agile and frequently speaks about her experiences at conferences across the globe. In 2015 Em became one of the first five people in the world to be certified as a SAFe 4.0 Program Consultant Trainer (SPCT4). Em is also the author of one of the 100 Top Agile blogs of 2015: PrettyAgile.com.

Contacting Em

Email: em@prettyagile.com

Blog: www.prettyagile.com

Follow Em on Twitter: @PrettyAgile

Connect with Em on LinkedIn:
https://au.linkedin.com/in/ejcampbellpretty